A.H. Sayce

Assyrian Grammar and Reading Book

A.H. Sayce

Assyrian Grammar and Reading Book

ISBN/EAN: 9783337243890

Printed in Europe, USA, Canada, Australia, Japan

Cover: Foto ©Andreas Hilbeck / pixelio.de

More available books at **www.hansebooks.com**

ARCHAIC CLASSICS.

ASSYRIAN GRAMMAR,

AND

READING BOOK.

AN

ELEMENTARY GRAMMAR;

WITH

FULL SYLLABARY

AND PROGRESSIVE READING BOOK,

OF

THE ASSYRIAN LANGUAGE,

IN THE

CUNEIFORM TYPE.

BY

THE REV. A. H. SAYCE, M.A.

FELLOW AND TUTOR OF QUEEN'S COLLEGE, OXFORD.

Author of "An Assyrian Grammar;" and "The Principles of Comparative Philology.

Multæ terricolis linguæ, cœlestibus una.

LONDON:

SAMUEL BAGSTER AND SONS,

15, PATERNOSTER ROW.

CONTENTS.

	PAGE
PREFACE	i
Syllabary	1
The Nouns	49
The Numerals	55
The Pronouns	57
The Verb	63
List of Prepositions	100
Compound Prepositions	102
The Conjunctions ...	103
The Adverbs ...	104
Derivation of Nouns	105
Phonology	106
Reading Lessons	108

PREFACE.

THE following pages have been written in connection with my lectures upon Assyrian philology, which were commenced in the early part of 1875 under the auspices of the Society of Biblical Archæology, and through the exertions of Mr. W. R. Cooper, the Secretary of the Society. An endeavour has been made for the first time to smooth over the difficulties which beset the entrance to the study of the Assyrian inscriptions, and so attract students to this new and important branch of research. When my " Assyrian Grammar" was published, three years ago, a knowledge of the language was still confined to the few, and there seemed little prospect that the small band of Assyriologues would be much increased for a long while to come. My work was therefore addressed to two classes of readers; to those who were already able to read the inscriptions, and could appreciate a grammar which entered into details and points of scholarship, and to those who were acquainted with the better-known Semitic languages, but wished to learn something of the new dialect which had been so unexpectedly revealed, and promised to throw such a flood of light on Semitic philology in general. The prospect, however, that three years ago seemed so distant has been more than realised. Assyrian has become a "popular" subject; and the world of scholars which once looked with distrust upon the labours of the decipherers, has at last awakened to their interest and importance. Students are flocking in from all sides, and elementary grammars and progressive reading-books, like those which initiate the pupil into Hebrew or Greek, are needed and called for.

The present volume is intended to meet this demand. The cuneiform type which has been freely used throughout will accustom the eye of the reader to the forms of the characters, and as all transliterated words are divided into syllables, even where the Assyrian text is not added, he will be able to reduce them into their original forms. Care has been taken not to burden the memory with unnecessary matter; and practical experience has proved that tabular lists of nouns, verbs, and particles, such as are given in the second part of the book, are the best means for impressing the rudiments of a new language upon the mind. A separate chapter on the syntax has been omitted, since any attempt to enter into details would be inconsistent with the plan of the Grammar, while it has been found more convenient to state those few cases of importance in which Assyrian differs from the syntactical usage of other languages in those places of the accidence to which they naturally belong. The notes appended to each of the reading-lessons are designed to lead the student on to a more advanced and independent acquaintance with the language, and so complete the work of a practical and elementary grammar.

The main difficulty is the Syllabary, the larger part of which will sooner or later have to be learnt by heart. The beginner is advised first to commit to memory the characters which express open syllables, given in pp. 46 and 47, as well as the Determinative Prefixes and Affixes given in p. 48, and then to work at the *monosyllabic* closed syllables. Experience alone can show him what are the commoner and more favourite values with which a character is used; and he must be content to be continually a learner, keeping the Syllabary constantly at his side for purposes of reference, and remembering that any endeavour to learn the *whole* Syllabary is a needless and useless task. He will soon come to know what characters and what values are most frequently employed, and what ideographs are most likely to occur in the inscriptions.

The hieroglyphic origin of the Syllabary, and its adaptation to the wants of a foreign language, will give the key to many of the difficulties he will meet with. Its Accadian inventors spoke an agglutinative dialect; and each hieroglyphic, which in course of time came to be corrupted into a cuneiform character (like the modern Chinese), originally expressed the sound of the word denoting the object or idea for which it stood. The same picture could stand for more ideas than one, and might therefore be pronounced in more than one way, so that when the Semitic Assyrians (or rather Babylonians) borrowed the cuneiform system of writing, using what were words in Accadian as mere phonetic values, polyphony became inevitable, and the same character represented several phonetic powers. Even in Accadian the characters could be employed phonetically as well as ideographically; and the Assyrians, while turning the dictionary of the Accadians into a huge syllabary, did not forget the hieroglyphic origin of the writing, but reserved to themselves the power of using a character not only as the representative of a syllabic sound, but also as an ideograph to which of course a Semitic pronunciation was attached.

Many of the characters exhibit their primitive form at the first glance; ⌐ for instance, clearly standing for "the tongue of a balance." In other cases the resemblance to the objects originally signified is not very visible in the simplified forms of the characters as used in Assyria, and we have to go back to the archaic Babylonian type to detect the likeness. Thus ◁ᐅ has lost all resemblance to "the sun;" and it is not until we remember the archaic ⊂⊃ that we discover the circle which stood for the great luminary of day. A large number of characters are compound, and when they are used ideographically their meaning can often be determined by considering what is the meaning of the separate characters of which they are made up. Thus ⊷𝄆𝄇 is "a mouth," and 𐎹 "a drop of water;" the compound ⊷𝄆𝄇 therefore naturally denotes the act of "drinking." So, again, the Assyrian ⊷𝄇 "a month" is the simplified form of the archaic 𐎁, where ⟨⟨⟨ the numeral 30 (expressing the 30 days of the month), is placed within the circle of the sun.

The use of polyphones no doubt increases the difficulty of decipherment, but the student will find that practically it is not so embarrassing as it would seem at first sight to be. The Assyrians intended their inscriptions to be read (at all events except in the case of texts like those of the astrological tablets, which were addressed to the initiated only), and accordingly adopted all possible means of obviating the disadvantages of a polyphonic system of writing. The following rules should be observed by the student in selecting one of the many values a given character may bear :—

(1) The existence of an ideograph should never be assumed, unless it is indicated by a phonetic complement, or unless the inscription (like the astrological ones generally) is written throughout ideographically rather than phonetically.

(2) Where two characters come together (such as *ca* and *ac*), the first of which ends with the same vowel as that with which the second begins, we may infer that they form one closed syllable (as *cac*).

(3) If a character expresses an open syllable (as *ri*) as well as a closed one (as *tal*), the open is to be preferred to the closed (unless contra-indicated).

(4) Those values are to be selected which offer a triliteral (or biliteral) root, and not a pluriliteral one.

(5) Notice must be taken of the final or initial consonant of the character which precedes or follows the one we are considering, as the Assyrians frequently doubled a consonant to show what value is to be chosen in a doubtful case. Thus ⟨cuneiform⟩ ⟨cuneiform⟩ must be read *dan-nin*, as *dan* alone out of the many possible values of the first character ends with *n*.

(6) A character which denotes a syllable beginning with a vowel is very rarely used after one which ends with a consonant.

(7) Words and lines end together, and proper names, &c., are pointed out by Determinative Prefixes and Affixes.

(8) Variant readings and variant forms of the same root must be carefully observed, as they often decide the pronunciation of a word where all other means fail.

(9) Experience will show that common use had set apart one or two values of a given character which were preferably employed to all others.

(10) Those values must be adopted which bring out a correct grammatical form, or enable us to compare the Assyrian word (should the context determine its meaning) with a similar root in the cognate languages.

It is not so much the existence of polyphones, however, that forms the chief defect in the Assyrian mode of writing. The phonology of the inventors of the writing was not the same as the phonology of the Assyrians, and sounds which were distinct in Assyrian had to be represented by one and the same sign. ⟨cuneiform⟩ is both *hu* or *u* (הו and או and ו) and *yu* (יו), ⟨cuneiform⟩ *za* and *tsa*, ⟨cuneiform⟩ *da* and *dha*, ⟨cuneiform⟩ *di* and *dhi*, ⟨cuneiform⟩ *e* (ע) and a modified י, ⟨cuneiform⟩ *bu* and *pu*. Similarly the same characters denoted both *m* and *v*, and no distinction was made between final *d*, *dh*, and *t*; *b* and *p*; *g*, *c*, and *k*; and *z*, *s*, *ts*, and even *s*; while closed syllables might begin as well as end with any of these doubtful letters. The uncertainty which results from this as to the initial or final letter of a syllable would naturally not press upon the Assyrian ; but it is the main difficulty against which the modern decipherer has to contend, and can only be overcome by the examination of new texts and the comparison of numerous passages.

A. H. SAYCE.

Queen's College, Oxford, April, 1875.

ASSYRIAN GRAMMAR.

SYLLABARY.

The characters of the Assyrian Syllabary were originally hieroglyphics, representing objects and ideas. The words by which these were denoted in the Turanian language of the Accadian inventors of the cuneiform system of writing became phonetic sounds when it was borrowed by the Semitic Assyrians, though the characters could still be used ideographically as well as phonetically. When used ideographically the pronunciation was, of course, that of the Assyrians.

In the following table only the forms of the characters found on the majority of the Assyrian monuments are given. Sometimes the so-called Hieratic characters were employed (*e.g.*, in the Cyprian Stele of Sargon) which differ but slightly from the Babylonian. Ancient Babylonian varied again in the forms of several characters. The Elamite or Susianian characters have the same form as the ancient Babylonian, while the Protomedic are modified from the Assyrian.

The Assyrian word in the right-hand column is a translation of the Accadian word (used in Assyrian as a phonetic value) in the left-hand column, and was the sound given to the character in the Assyrian inscriptions whenever it was read as an ideograph.

Phonetic Value (Accadian word).	Cuneiform Character.	Assyrian rendering.	Meaning.
1. as	➤━	magaru, dilu ...	*obedient (happy)*, ?
ruv (rum, ru)	,,	zicaru, dilu	*a male*, ?
dil	,,	nabu, dilu	*to proclaim*, ?
	,,	estin, khidu, edisu ...	*one*
	,,	namkullû	?
	,,	ina	*in*
	,,	Assur (*an abbreviation*)	*Assyria*
kharra ...	,,	samu, tuhamtu ...	*heaven, the deep*

2

Phonetic Value (Accadian word).	Cuneiform Character.	Assyrian rendering.	Meaning.
2. khal	►►►─	nacaśu, buligu ...	*to cut, division*
khas	,,	khasu	*?*
khal	,,	gararu ...	*to roll stormily*
	,,	pulukhu ...	*reverence*
	,,	zuzu... ...	*a fixture*
3. ? ...	►►►─	[sumunesrit] ...	*eighteen*
4. an, ana ...	►►─Y	sakū, samū, ilu, Anu,	*high, sky, god, the god Anu*
anna, annab...	,,	sakū, samū, ilu, Anu,	*high, sky, god, the god Anu*
dimir, dingir...	,,	ilu	*god*
sa	,,	cacabu	*star*
essa	,,	ilutu sa sibri ...	*divinity of corn*
an	,,	supultu	*depth*
4a. nab (see 168)	𒀯	nabbu ...	*divinity*
4b. simidan ...	►Y─𒅗	nalbar-same... ...	*the zenith*
4c. alat, alap ...	►Y─ ═YY►Y	sēdu	*spirit (divine bull)*
4d. lamma ...	►Y─ ═YYY	lamaśśu ...	*colossus*
alap (*Ass. val.*)	,,	buhidu ...	*colossus*
5. khaz (khas, khats)	►►─	nadu, nacaśu ...	*to place, to cut*
kut (kud) ...	,,	nacaśu, gazaru ...	*to cut, to cut*
tar	,,	nacaśu, danu, sāmu	*to cut, to judge, to set*
sil (śil, śila) ...	,,	sūku, panu	*canal, before*
gug, citamma	,,		
	,,	sallatu, halacu, eribu	*spoil, to go, to descend (flow)*
6. pal	►═Y◄	ebiru, etiku, palu, napalcutu, nucuru, palu	*to cross, to pass through, time or year, to revolt, enemy, sword*
tal	,,	ebiru, etiku	*to cross, to pass through*
pal	,,	supilu sa sinnis, pukhkhu sa sinnis, supiltu	*sexual part of a woman, sexual part of a woman, the lower part*
nuk (?) ...	,,	nakū...	*to sacrifice*
zabur... ...	,,	admu, akhri, khiru ...	*man, behind, lord*

Phonetic Value (Accadian word).	Cuneiform Character.	Assyrian rendering.	Meaning.
7. bat, be ...		pagru, pitu, mutu, labiru, uduntu	corpse, to open, to die, old, ?
til, badhdhu ...	,,	gamaru, pagru, katu	complete, corpse, hand
us	,,	dāmu	blood (offspring)
khar	,,		
ziz(?), mit, idim	,,		
	,,	nakbu, samu, captu, belu, enuva, tsēru	channel, heaven, heavy, lord, when, desert
8. lugud ...		sarsu ...	omen of good
9. adama ...		adamatu ...	omen of evil
10. susru... ...		ussusu ...	founder (surname of Anu)
11. gir		sumuk-same, padhru	vault of heaven, to strike
rum	,,	littu, padhru ...	sword, point
gir	,,	girū, zukabulbu, padanu, birku	point, ?, plain, lightning
12. pur, pul ...		passaru	to explain (?)
du, gim ...	,,	edissu, sumnu ...	alone, fat
mucmuc-nabi	,,		solitary
usu	,,	edisu	sweet odour, desert (?), to sell
	,,	basmu, butu, macaru, garru	or exchange, expedition (?)
13. kur		naciru, sannu, pappu	to change, enemy, other (?)
pap	,,	pappu, zicaru, tarbu, natsaru, akhu	other (?), male, young man, to defend, brother
13a. *khal, dili-dili-nabi ...		itallucu ...	a path
gisi-u-khallacu	,,	pusku ...	difficult road (?)
14. utuci		samsu ...	the Sun
15. zubu		gamlu ...	benefit
gam	,,	sicru... ...	kindness
16. taltal... ...		Ea	the god Hea

Phonetic Value (Accadian word).	Cunciform Character.	Assyrian rendering.	Meaning.
17. zicura ...		citim ...	*lower* or *beneath*
18. cit, cuda, se ..		epikhu, carasu ...	*to blow, property (standard, camp)*
	"	calū, ezibu, patā ...	*the whole, to leave, to open*
śabura ...	"	cupkhu	?
gudibir ...	"	Maruducu	*Merodach*
tak	"		
19. seslam ...		cipratu ...	*race* or *region*
20. ka, gita ...			determinative of measure
21. cit (kit, cat) ...		salamu ...	*to accomplish*
22. ru, sub ...		idu, nadanu, takku, raddu, cabadu, pakadu	*to know, to give, ?, to add, to oppress* or *be multitudinous, to oversee*
u, ub, bu ...	"	itsbu ...	?
23. mu		sumu, santu, zicaru, nadanu, ya, samu	*name, year, memorial, to give, my, sky*
	"	masaddu, cu'aśu, khalacu, cuśśu, vācu	*?, ?, ?, throne, ?*
nurma ...	"		
23a. ? ...		idlutu ...	*strength*
24. nu		la, (ul), tsalamu ...	*not, image*
patesi ...	"	zicaru	*male (viceroy)*
25. kul (*Assyrian value* zir)		ziru	*seed*
26. zir ...		nūru... ...	*light (meteor)*
27. na		zicaru, annu, samu, makhirtu	*memorial, this, sky, front*
28. ti, til, tsil ...		baladhu, napistu, naśu	*family, life, to raise*
	"	lakū, tsabatu, dakhu	*to take, to seize, to be near*
	"	usibu, dapanu-sa-ru-cubi, anbu, tsilu	*dwell, side* (or *wheel*) *of a chariot, ?, side*

Phonetic Value (Accadian word).	Cuneiform Character.	Assyrian rendering.	Meaning.
29. uru, eri ...		ālu ...	a city (tent)
30. uru		ālu, abubu ...	city, heap of corn
31. erim		isittu ...	a foundation
32. sek		sakummatu ...	a summit
33. gur		caśamu ...	?
34. sacir, saciśa ...			?
35. ukki		uku, pukhru ...	people, assembly
36. uru, gisgal ... mulu		ālu, manzazu ... nisu	city, fortress man
37. silik		sagaburu ...	strong protector, rank
38. sucit (?) (See No. 197b.)		passuru ...	Lenormant "kind of parasol"
38a. kal, gar ...		?	?
39. ca, gu, cir, du, zu, cagu ...		pū, amatu, appu, pānu, inu, uznu, bunnu, makhru, sepu, amaru, amanu, kābu, sāsu, ricmu, saganu, cibu, mātu	mouth, fealty, face, face, eye, ear, form, front, foot, sight, completion, to speak, ?, push, ?, mass, country (properly face of the country)
duk	,,	ilu sa napkhari, erisu	god of the universe, to ask
gu, cagu ...	,,	calu, saku sa me, canicu	all, drinking of water, seal
ca	,,	ricim, sunnu, idculu	blow, a half, confidence (?)
39a. duddhu ...		dabibu, pālu, idacculu	deviser, ?, ?
39b. gude ...		nabu, khababu, nagagu	proclaimer, lover (?), ?
39c. śidi, śiśi ...		urrikhtu ...	?

Phonetic Value (Accadian word).	Cunciform Character.	Assyrian rendering.	Meaning.
39d. cimmu ...		sipru, dhemu ...	explanation, law
40. me		takhatsu ...	battle
41. impar ...		...	glory (name)
42. cmi		lisānu ...	tongue (language)
43. ?		saptu ...	lip (sentence)
44. ? ...		saptu, tsumu ...	lip, thirst
45. ? ...		tsumu ...	thirst (fast)
46. cu ...		acalu, khadhdhu ...	to eat, food (חרם)
47. mû ...		camu ...	to burn (?)
48. ? ...		pukhkhu ...	the breath
49. ?		tsalamtu ...	darkness
50. ibira		damkaru (of Acc. origin)	?
51. ? ...		ikhimu ...	he burnt (devoured)
51a. ? ...		? ...	?
52 ?		? ...	?
53. ? ...		? ...	?
54. bat		imtu...	poison (philtre)
55. ? ...		? ...	terror
56. ? ...		? ...	?
57. nak		satu	to drink
58. ? ...		uru	city
59. la ...		laluru, khazbu ...	?; ?

Phonetic Value (Accadian word).	Cuneiform Character.	Assyrian rendering.	Meaning.
60. tu ...	⊱𝍣𝍦, ⟪⊱𝍦	cribu, śummatu ...	*to descend* or *enter* or *set* (of the Sun), *season* (?)
turi, tura ...	,,	eribu, murtsu ...	*to descend, &c., sickness*
61. li ...	⊱𝍣𝍦𝍦, ⊱𝍣⟨, ⟪⊱𝍦⟨	rāru, liliśu	?, ?
(*note these variant forms*)			
gub, gu ...	,,	illu	*high* or *precious*
ni	,,		
62. apin, pin, uru	⊱𝍣𝍦	epinu, ussu	*foundation* (*city*)
engar ...	,,	iccaru	*ground* (*digging*)
63. makh ...	⊱𝍣𝍦𝍦	tsiru, makhkhu (*from Acc.*), rubū, mahdu	*supreme, supreme, great, much*
	,,	bahalu, tublu, tizkaru	*prince* (?), *sovereign* (?), ?
64. bar, mas ...	✛	paratsu, burru, bāru, usuru, tsindu, akhratu, akhkhuru, tsātu, rikātu, akhatu, akhu, akhitu, arcu, tsabiu	*to divide, half, half, bound, to bind, another, after, future, future, a second, brother, other, after, gazelle*
	,,	camātu, gabbi, tinū, enitu, pisaktu, cabitu, mala, palaśu, tuhāmu, zibtu, dallu, ciśittu, niśu, ruzzu, elitu, śanku, makhazu, bidhru, asaridu, pulu, maru, bidhramu, ibbu, libutu, amaru, masū, vassaru, zumru, cabadtu	*heap* (?), *all,* ?, ?, *oracle, much, as many as, to weigh,* ?, ?, *the Tigris,* ?, ?, ?, *upper, chain, battle, firstborn* (?), *eldest, cattle, son, firstborn* (?), *white,* ?, *to see,* ?, *to abandon, body, the liver*
mas	,,	māsu, Adaru, asibu, ellu, tsabitu, māzu-sa-ecili	?, *the god Adar, to dwell, high* (*precious*), *to take, burning* (?) *of a field*
śa	,,		
65. rat, sit ...	⊱𝍦𝍦⊱	radhu	?

Phonetic Value (Accadian word).	Cuneiform Character.	Assyrian rendering.	Meaning.
66. nun ... ... zil, sil, humis, khan (?)	▶️YY▶-, ▶-YYY, ▶-YYYY „	rubū, rabu, nunu, (fr. Acc.)	prince, great, prince
66a. asagara ...	▶-YYYY YY<	asagaru	a hurricane
67. tur, silam (?)...	▶-YYY< T Y, ▶-YYY<∗ Y	tarbatsu	rest or eclipse
68. silam, akar ...	▶-YYY<Y₸Y	? ...	reverence (?)
69. biru (perhaps Ass.)	▶-Y◁	suttu, uritsu, tsiptu, nipikhu	dream, offspring, product, revenue
70. cun	▶-Y◁▶-YYY	zibbatu, zumbu ...	tail, tail
71. ? ...	▶-Y◁Y	?	?
72. ? ...	▶-Y◁Y	?	?
73. khu, pak ... khu, pak, musen	▶-YY, ▶-Y<Y „	itstsuru, śaru ... musennu	bird, king (?) ?
74. pacac ...	▶-YY ₸	ciribu, sumelu ...	middle, left hand
75. śa	▶-YY<◁₸₸	nabū ...	to proclaim
76. ik	▶-Y<Y◁	iku (or ikku), daltu, khamdhu, patu, nukhsu	?, door, quick journey, to open, prosperity
gal	„	basū, sacunu, nasu, labinu	to be, placed, to raise, brick
gal	„	ikku, rutstsunu, malū, asabu, pitū, cānu, natsaru	?, ?, to fill, to dwell, to open, to establish, to defend
77. tsim, zim, nam (Acc. prefix of abstract noun) nam	▶-YY✕ . „ „	simtu, sakhalu ... nabu, śimmu ... nammu, pikhatu, mā	destiny, plague (?) to proclaim, destiny ?, a governor, this
78. pak (?) ...	▶-YY✕ <Y	itstsuru ...	a bird

Phonetic Value (Accadian word).	Cuneiform Character.	Assyrian rendering.	Meaning.
79. mut	▶〉◁	banū, dāmu, uppu, aladu, icbu, bisru, barradu	*to create, blood, ?, to bear children, ?, flesh, seed*
musendugusi	”		
80. zi ...	▶〉✦	napistu, nisu, pilū, nasakhu, dikū, būā, saparu	*life (soul), man (spirit), work, to take away, smitten, to come, to send*
81. gi, sa... ...	▶〉◁	kanū, duppu-sadhru, simtu, zicaru, mātu, esiri, tāru, gimiru, pudak, cunu	*reed, written tablet, foundation, memorial, country, bands, to restore, all, ?, established*
81a. caradin ...	▶〉◁ ▢▢	cissu ...	*multitudinous*
82. ? ...	▶〉◁✦	? ...	*?*
83. ri, tal ...	▶〉〉, ▶〉〈〉	tallu, ramū, lilu, tsakku, parasu-sarikhuti, parsidu	*mound, height, ?, ?, ?, to fly away*
di	”	nabadhu	*brilliance*
es	”	nadū	*brightness (of a star)*
sa	”	saruru	*the firmament*
84. gub	▶〉〉, 〈〉〈〉	sumelu	*left hand*
kat	..	gubbu (*of Accadian origin*)	*left hand*
85. tun, khub ...	▶〉✦〉, ▶〉✦〉	khasu	*?*
86. pulug ...	▶〉〉▶✦	carasu sa etsi ...	*implement of wood*
87. ac, gar ...	▶▢, ▶〉▣	episu, banū, makharu, nabu, Nabū, khasisu, pit-uzni, rapsa-uzni, khubbu-sakani	*to make, to build, to be present, to proclaim, Nebo, the intelligent, the opener of the ears, the enlarger of the ears, hollow of a reed*
ac ...	”	belu... ...	*lord*
88. me	▶✦▶〉	takhatsu	*battle*
89. sus	▶▢〉〉	?	*?*

Phonetic Value (Accadian word).	Cuneiform Character.	Assyrian rendering.	Meaning.
90. ? ...		? ...	?
91. cum, kum ...		citu	*linen*
91a. *sa		gallabu	*sleeve* (?)
91b. sinik ...		bīnu... ...	?
92. ? ...		tsupuru ...	*nail (nail-mark)*
? ...	,,	simmu ...	*destruction*
92a. ? ...		kharru ...	?
92b. sacil ...		cillu... ...	?
92c. tabin [or ebin], gadataccuru		tsupru, masaru, tsumbu, ubanu, imdhu	*nail, to leave* (?), *tail* (?), *peak, staff* (?)
93. dim, tim, tiv, tï		ricśu, riciś-kanē, marcaśu, timmu	*bond, bundle of reeds, cable, rope*
94. mun (munu)...		dhabtu ...	*benefit*
95. pulug (from Assn.)		pulugu ...	*division* or *choice*
96. en ...		belu, enu ...	*lord, lord*
	,,	adi	*up to*
enu	,,	samu ...	*sky*
97. dara		turakhu ...	*antilope*
	,,	Ea	*the god Ea*
98. mu		sumu ...	*name*
99. sur (zur) ...		zamaru, zarakhu, tsaruru, naśakhu - sa - amati, ridu, khabsu, capalu, zunnu, summa, basu	*to make go forth, to rise, body (or rising), removal of anything, servant, trodden down* (?), ?, *rain, thus, to exist*
100. sukh (śukh)		pultu, mātu, naparcu, zimu, pallu, nasaku, tihamtu	?, *country, to break, glory*, ?, *to climb, the sea*
tiskhu ...	,,	ramcuti ...	*herd* [or *stay*?]

Phonetic Value (Accadian word).	Cuneiform Character.	Assyrian rendering.	Meaning.
101. śucus		Istar. .	the goddess Istar
102. se,sakh(śakh), nakh, nikh		surbu	prince
103. ba		episu, banū, zuzu, ciśu, nasaru, csiru, su, pitu	to make, to create, to fix, a sword, ?, a shrine, he, to open
104. zu, la		lamadu, raddu, idū, mudu, ca, nindanu	to learn, to add, to know, wise, thy, a gift
104a. abzu		abzū	the abyss
105. śu, sir		zumuru, tsuru, masacu, rabā	a body, ?, skin, to increase
106. sun (śun)		gablu	front (middle, battle)
107. muk		muccu	a building
107a. mukmuk-nabi		basmu	altar of incense
108. zadim		śaśinu	plant (?)
109. nit (nitakh, nita), cri		zicaru, ardu…	man, slave
110. idu, itu		arkhu	month
111. sakh, sukh		damaku, dabu, sakhu	prosperous, a bear, tiger
112. sibir…		sibru, kharpu	corn, crop
113. gur …		tāru, śacibu, basu, naçru-sa-amati	to restore, ?, to be (become), breaker of faith
114. dar … dar, śi-gunū		tarru, birmi, atsu … litu, sutruru, pitsu …	?, variegated cloths, growth offspring, white, white
115. ?		?	"flask, languishing" (M. Lenormant)

Phonetic Value (Accadian word).	Cuneiform Character.	Assyrian rendering.	Meaning.
116. śa, pa	𒐀	latnu, masadu, markaśu, bu'anu	?, ?, *firmament (bond), ulcer*
[śa-gitu]	"		
117. gis (?)	𒐀	samu	*the sky*
118. śi	𒐀	karnu, malu, giru, enisu, śamu, issaccu, dussu, itanu, pitu, cunnu, samu	*horn, to fill, enemy (or campaign), man, blue, prince, ?, ?, to open, established, sky*
śig	"	malū	*to fill (give)*
118a. śicca	𒐀	atudu	*he-goat*
119. śa'ib	𒐀	'urukhkhu	*road*
120. śi, (śe) (sometimes confused with dar)	𒐀	gunnu, calu, pilū, pilutu, bitru, atsu-sa-etsi-u-kani	*garden, entrails (kidneys), choice, choice, ?, growth of trees and grass*
121. mā	𒐀	clippu	*a ship*
122. uz, mus	𒐀	enzu	*goats' hair*
123. * * ur	𒐀	calū naccalu	*a complete vessel*
124. ticul, dellu dimśun	𒐀	sukkullu, acū	*intelligence, ?*
125. surru	𒐀	surrū, calū	*beginning (?), vessel*
126. guana	𒐀	kablu	*middle*
127. ?	𒐀	cratu	*pregnant*
128. dir	𒐀, 𒐀	adru, khalabu, sutruru, khibu, mikid-isati	*dark, white, covered, wanting, burning of fire*
śa	"	śamu	*blue*
pir	"	saku-sa-nisi	*head of a man*
dak	"	nikhabbu, malu, ikubbu	*covering, to fill, vault*
129. maś, (alat)	𒐀	tsabu, alapu	*soldier, warrior spirit (bull)*

Phonetic Value (Accadian word).	Cuneiform Character.	Assyrian rendering.	Meaning.
130. sak (ris *in* Ass.)		risu, karnu, śangu, panu, rabu, avilu, pukhu	*head, horn, chain, face, great, man, ?*
130a. sakus ...		saku-sa-risi, asaridu...	*top of the head, eldest*
130b. eśśat ...		? ...	?
131. mukh ...		mukhkhu	*brain (?)*
132. ? ...		? ...	?
133. uru		zicaru ...	*male*
134. aru		nestu ...	*female*
135. gudhu ...		karradu ...	*hero*
136. can		adaru, adirtu ...	*dark, eclipse*
137. tab (tap) ...		tsabatu, tamakhu, ezibu, sitenu, uraddu, tabbu	*to seize, to hold, to leave, double (?), to add (give back), double*
dili-dili-nabi	„	surru, napkharu ...	*beginning, totality*
138. rû (ra) ...		banu	*to make*
kak	„	episu, cala	*to make, all*
	„	siccatu, rapdu ...	*door (?), ?*
dû, gag (*sometimes in Ass.* cal)	„	banu, danu ...	*to create, to judge*
139. ni, ne ...		yahu [*or* i]	*to be (?)*
zal (zalli), ili	„	yahu...	*to be (?)*
	„	akhkhuru, namaru, masu, zicaru, azalu, narabu, nakhu, sunku-sa-niz. ciśallu	*presence, to see, week (?), man, to depart, ?, to rest (?), want of *, altar*
140. ili		imin nabi	?
141. ir		salalu	*to spoil*
sucal ...	„	sucallu	*fruit*

Phonetic Value (Accadian word).	Cuneiform Character.	Assyrian rendering.	Meaning.
142. mal,.ma, c ... gal, gā, pi-śannu	𒈗	bitu, sacanu ...	*house, to establish*
ilba ...	,,	saracu, maru, callu ...	*to give, young, to restrain*
143. gusur ...		gusuru, idlu... ...	*beam, hero*
144. cisal ...		ciśallu ...	*altar*
145. ? ...		? ...	?
146. nen, lucu, ekhi		ummu ...	*mother*
ismal ...	,,	rapsu ...	*large*
147. ? ...		ummu ...	*mother*
148. gapi... ...		? ...	?
149. ? ...		alittu	*generatrix*
150. ega		agu	*crown*
151. ? ...		remu ...	*mercy*
152. ? ...		remu ...	*grace*
153. gan (gana) gāgunū		iclu, padanu, ginu, nabadhu	*field, plain, enclosure (garden), light*
gāgunū ...	,,	khaśaśu	*intelligent (to determine)*
car	,,	sapalu, caru... ...	*lower, fortress*
aganateti ...	,,	nasû...	*to raise*
154. dak... ...		napaldhu, rapadu ,...	*to survive, ?*
bara (par) ...	:,	sutruru, adannu ...	*covered, a season*
155. ciśim, zibin, surin, sarin		ciśimmu, nabbillu, tsatsiru, sikhu	*different kinds of locusts*
kharub (*from Ass.*)	,,	kharubu, zirbabu ...	*a locust, do.*
156. agan, ubir ...		tulu, tsirtu	*a mound, tent (?)*
157. amas, śubura		śuburu	*darkness*

Phonetic Value (Accadian word).	Cuneiform Character.	Assyrian rendering.	Meaning.
158. us, nita, nitakh, dhūcus ...		emidu, zicaru, ridu, mutstsu, nitakhu, isaru, rikhu, abadu	to stand, man, servant, offspring, man, phallus, smell(?), ?
159. kas		sinātu ...	urine
160. tak		abnu, saku-sa-icli ...	stone, top of a field
161. tik, gū ...		makhru, mekhitstu, cisadu, mātu, napkharu	front, battle, neighbourhood (bank), country, totality
161a. izcun ...		etsen-tsiru	tip of the tail
161b. muśup ...		nasu-sa-resi, saku-saresi	lifting of the head, top of the head
162. gun... ...		biltu... ...	tribute (a talent)
163. dhur (dur) ...		karnu ...	a crescent
164. ? ...		eru	copper
165. hubisega ...		Bilu... ...	Bel
166. sana (sa) (read irba in Ass.)		irbu	four
167. ab (ap, abba) es	,,	abtu, esu, tamtu ... bitu, kabu	?, ?, the sea house, hollow (?)
168. nab (nap) (see 4a)		nuru... ...	light
169. mul, ana-essecu		caccabu, nabadhu ...	star, brightness
170. tak (tag), sum, nas sum... ... tak, suridu ...	,, ,,	labanu, libitu, lapatu, bāru, naclu dabakhu ... ... zuhunu, labatsu, makhatsu - sa - ali, śalatsu, bāru, sālu, nabatsu, nadu	brick, omen, hinge (?), lake (?), complete to cut the throat (sacrifice) plenty (?), ?, stronghold of a city, ?, lake (?), ?, ?, situated

Phonetic Value (Accadian word).	Cuneiform Character.	Assyrian rendering.	Meaning.
171. cā	𒁉	bābu ...	*gate*
172. az (ats, aś) ...	𒊍	atsu	?
173. uk (ug) ...	𒊏	immu [*or* tammu], ucu	*day* [or *paragon*], *great* (?)
174. um, mus ... dikh ... dub, dib (duppa)	𒌝, 𒌝 " "	ummu, libu, dabacu abnu, canacu-sa-abni lāvu, dippu, tsabatu, lavū, sapacu, tabacu, saraku, tuppu, tsipu	?, ?, *to cleave to stone, signet tablet, document, to seize, to approach, to heap up, to heap up, to be red* (?), ?, *produce* (?)
175. śumuk ...	𒋳	sūtu	*library* (?)
176. śamak ...	𒈬	mutstsatu ...	*library*
177. urud (urudu)	𒍐	cru	*bronze*
178. Ninua (?) ...	𒌷, 𒌷	Ninua ...	*Nineveh* (literally *bronze fish*)
179. i, i-gittū ... khi	𒄿 "	nahidu, naku, atsu-sa-samsi khu	*clear* (*glorious*), *pure, sunrise glorious* (?)
180. gan, can (kan) kam ...	𒃶 "	annu, nagabu, basu, su, khagalu *	*cloud* (?), *canal, to be, he* (*this*), *to irrigate* forms ordinal numbers
181. ad (at) ...	𒀜	abu	*father* (*king*)
182. tsi	𒍝	martu ...	*west* (?)
183. ya	𒐊	naku ...	*pure*
184. tur ... dū	𒌉 "	zakhru, maru, karradu ablu, maru	*small, young, young warrior son, son*
185. ginna, khibiz	𒅔	muniru ...	*overwhelmer*
186. ibila (*borrowed from Ass.*)	𒉽 𒉽	ablu	*son*

Phonetic Value (Accadian word).	Cuneiform Character.	Assyrian rendering.	Meaning.
187. turrak ...		bintu, martu ...	*daughter, woman*
188. turrak ...		bintu ...	*daughter*
189. dumugu ...		samsu ...	*the sun-god*
190. ta, nas (*See* 205)		ina, ultu ...	*in, from*
191. ? ...		iclitu ...	*darkness (prison)*
192. in		innu, biltu, śilu, pillu	*lord (?), mastery, rock (?), ?*
193. un-gal, lu-gal sar (*borrowed from Ass.*)		śarru, śaru	*king, monarch*
194. rab, raba (rap) dim ...		rabbu ...	?
195. dim... ...		macutu, labartu ...	*a path (?), a phantom*
196. cib (cip, kip)		?	?
197. bi, cas (kas), ul		sane, sannu, su, suātu, nakbu	*two, second, he, this, channel*
cas	,,	cāsu (*borrowed from Acc.*)	*double*
197a. kharran ...		khammu ...	*a quarter of the sky (point of the compass)*
197b. sucit (?) ...		passuru ...	*royal parasol (?)*
198. ? ...		kharatsu ...	*to make*
199. cas (kas), ras		kharranu (durgu), sane, rabadhu	*road, two, ?*
kharran ...	,,		
cas-cal ...	,,	kharranu (*from Acc.*)	*road*
200. illat... ...		illat	?
201. rutu ...		rutu	*troops*

Phonetic Value (Accadian word).	Cuneiform Character.	Assyrian rendering.	Meaning.
202. gur		namandu	*measure* (?)
ninda ...	„	ittū	*a sign*
203. ? ...		?	"*abundance, generosity*" (Lenormant)
204. is (iśi), mil, mis		sadu, urru	*mountain (heap), light*
śakhar ...	,	'ipru, bisśatu ...	*dust, mud*
	„	summa	*thus (if)*
205. ? (*See* 190)		?	"*to begin*" (Lenormant)
206. rim, cabar, im		sulū, sanu(tu) ...	*mound, seconde*(?)
207. sim, rik, śiriz		sammu ...	*price (income)*
208. ?		?	?
208. ? ...		nacmu ...	*a captive*
209. ku, kum, ri ...		saku, khasalu ...	*top, to destroy*
210. ur		isittu, cipśu-sa-nisi, uzunu, udlu	*foundation (the nadir), testicle, equal weight, level ground*
211. il, cacaśiga ...		?	?
212. du (dun) ...		alacu, alacu-khamdhu, tahalu - khamdhu, licu - khamdhu, alacu-maru	*to go, a swift journey, a swift onset, a swift march, a little journey*
gub	„	nazazu	*to fix (to wax of* the moon)
gin, aradupū	„	nazuzu, basu, alacu, cānu, saparu, magaru, anacu	*to be fixed, to exist, to go, to establish, to send, to love, I*
sa, ra, ir, gubba	„	aradubū	*pursue* (?)
		tsabatu, sapiru, calu, sulū	*to seize, messenger, all, mound*

Phonetic Value (Accadian word).	Cuneiform Character.	Assyrian rendering.	Meaning.
212a. aradudu-nabi		cānu, uzuzu, ceśu-sa-elappi, alacu-sa-cissati	to establish, fix, pain of the womb, marching of a multitude
213. gum, nitakh		rabu, nisu	an official, a man
214. **r		? ...	"to adhere" (Lenormant)
215. rim		iśdu, sulu	foundation, heap
216. rik, khil ...		? ...	?
217. gesdin ...		caranu ...	goat [or vine]
218. ib (ip) ... tum (tuv, tu) urugal, aralli	" "	gablu, su, agagu ... khardatu ... ... mitu...	middle, he, ? fear death (Hades)
219. egir... ... aba	"	arcu (arcatu) ...	after
220. paz (?) ...		'imiru ...	beast (ass), homer (a measure)
221. gis, nen (?)... iz (itz, iś) (Ass. value) gis	" "	etsu, zicaru, rabu, esiru samu ...	tree (wood), man, great, temple heaven
221a. gudhu ...		caccu, tugultu, bilu, gudhu	weapon, service (servant), lord, end
221b. alal ...		alallu, miśu, metsu ...	papyrus, ?, shoot (?)
222. pa, du (?) ... khut, khat, cun	"	aru, gappu, gisdaru... nahru-sa-yumi ...	?, wing, ? dayspring
222a. luga		surupu ...	burnt
222b. gistar, tirtar		tirtu, śuśaccu ...	form (body), ?
223. pu		graphic variant of sign	

Phonetic Value (Accadian word).	Cuneiform Character.	Assyrian rendering.	Meaning.
224. ·mar, nikh ...		marru, sacanu, nigganu, pada, radu, basu	path, to establish, enclosure, ?, descent, to exist
225. gc, cit ...		citu. zacicu	below, abyss
lil	,,	cītu	below
226. hu (u), sam		umu, ammatu ...	the same, a cubit
cus	,,	akhu, acalu	brother (?), to eat
227. ga, gur ... (forms adjectives in Accadian)		gu, tsarapu, tsamadu-sa-narcabti, ma-caru - sa - macuri, sizbu	?, purifier, chariot-yoke, cord for wares, ?
227a. ili		nasu, saku, makhru, guru	to raise, top, front, ?
228. lakh (lakhkha)		miśu	?
lakh, lukh, śun	,,	pasisu, ardu... ...	?, servant
succal, lukh nakh (in Susian)	,, ,,	succallu ...	intelligence (messenger)
229. al		allu	?
230. mis (miz), rid, lak		idlu, karā, śangu, cirbannu	hero, to call, chain, gift
cisip ...	,,	rittu	?
sit (siti) ...	,,	alittu, madadu, min utu, sadhru	genetrix, to measure, number, to write
ak	,,	idku	ring (?)
alal, piśan ...	,,	piśannu, natsabu-sa-etsi	papyrus, shaft of a tree
231. alal, dibbi-sak		natsabu-sa-kani, dup-pu-sadhru	shaft of a reed, written tablet
sak	,,	Nabū	the god Nebo
232. gut (gud), khar, dapara, lē		alpu, lū ...	bull, herd
telal	,,	ecimmu ...	bull-like demon

Phonetic Value (Accadian word).	Cuneiform Character.	Assyrian rendering.	Meaning.
233. cus, billudu		billudū	?
garza ...	„	partsu	captain (law)
234. mascim ...		rabitsu ...	an incubus
235. sabra ...		sabru ... ?	?
236. nuzcu ...		nuscu ...	Nuscu (identified with Nebo)
237. sib (śiba) ...		ri'u, belu ...	shepherd, lord
238. sab (sap), gistar-urassacu		sabbu, gablu, saramu	?, interior, to sacrifice
239. e ...		kābu, bitu, kabu ...	hollow, house, to speak
240. duk ...		sacunu	a building
lut	„	pulgu, carpatu ...	choice, ?
241. un		nisu	man
ucu	„	uku (from Acc.) ...	people
calama ...	„	matu ...	country
241. dan ...		dannu	strong
cal, gurus ...	„	asdhu, akru, dannu, egiru, asaridu	?, costly, mighty, to dig, eldest
lab, lib, rib ...	„	idlu	a warrior
gurus ...	„	gurusu, idlu ...	a warrior, a hero
zan, śim ...	„	mātu	country
242. am		rīmu ...	wild bull
243. uzu		sīru ...	flesh (limb, health)
244. ne, iz ...		isatu, napakhu ...	fire, to dawn
bi, bil, pil, gibil	„	kalū... ...	to burn
dhe ...	„	cararu, essetu, sussu	to revolve, new, sixty
cum (of Ass. origin)	„	camu	to burn

Phonetic Value (Accadian word).	Cuneiform Character.	Assyrian rendering.	Meaning.
245. gi, gibil ...		kalū, bu'idu... ...	*to burn, a spirit*
246. gil, śim ...		?, idguru ...	*"construction, wall, to glide"* (Lenormant)
247. guk		cibuśu, garru, mandinu	*trampling, expedition, gift (?)*
248. nir		śarru, malicu ...	*king, prince*
249. acar ...		aplukhtu ...	*reverence*
250. ub (up), ār (ara)		cipru, tupku, garmu, enakhu	*region, zone, quarter, to decay*
251. mebulug (*of Ass. origin*)		mebulugu, sabuccu...	*choice, ?*
252. gab, dū, takh		makharu, irtu, daku, padharu, padi, isi, dakhadu, nadhalu, naśikhu, etsibu, saninu, nadhalu	*front, breast, to strike, to deliver, ?, he has, to rejoice, to raise, a remover, to establish, a rival, to transfer*
takh ...	"	labanu-libanu ...	*brickwork*
	"	radu	*descent* (or *thunderbolt*)
253. zin ... ... zer (*of Ass. origin*)		tseru ...	*desert*
	"		
rabita ...	"	iztati ...	*?*
254. takh ...		etsibu, uraddu ...	*to establish, to dispose*
255. sam ...		simu ...	*price*
256. zik (zig), khas		zikku, sabru, garru ...	*?, to break, expedition (?)*
257. uru		aru, cpuru	*?, fecundity*
ugudili ...	"	esgurru	*?*
258. ?		?	*?*

Phonetic Value (Accadian word).	Cuneiform Character.	Assyrian rendering.	Meaning.
259. usbar		uspa-rabu	great quiver
uzu	„	barū... ...	?
260. urugal ...		gabru ...	opposer (hero)
261. sam... ...		? ...	?
262. aca		rāmu, nasu, madadu, maharu	high, to raise, to measure, to urge on
ram (Ass. value)	„		
263. ?		partsu ...	divider (?)
264. lab, rud ...		alu	city
265. agarin ...		umnu ...	mother (?)
266. ? ...		śarru ...	king
267. ubigi ...		? ...	shrine (?)
268. ? ...		? ...	?
269. gaz (gaza), bi		dāku, niku, puhuz, khibu	to smite, victim, ?, wanting (?)
270. lil, ubi ... galam, galum		abutu, śaru, naclu ...	charm, king, complete
271. ? ...		? ...	?
272. zicura ...		irtsitu ...	the earth
273. taltal ...		Ea	the god Ea
274. śi, ṣc, sem ...		nadanu, sacaru ... nadu, śapanu, idu, sāmu, palaśu	to give, to give to place, to sweep away, to lay, to set, to weigh (be favourable)
śi, śunnu ...	„	ananu-sa-*, lavu-sa-*	?, tablet of *

Phonetic Value (Accadian word).	Cuneiform Character.	Assyrian rendering.	Meaning.
275. rakh, ukhula		? ...	?
276. šar		sadhru, mušaru, sumu	to write, an inscription, name
khir, khur ...	,,	zarakhu, zamaru, da-rudu, atsu-sa-etsi-u-kani	to rise, to dawn, ?, growth of trees and grass
khir... ...	,,	arku, racišu, rucušu, ciru, calū, nabu, cašu	green, to bind, bond, enclosure, all, to proclaim, to cover
cismakh, * gū	,,	samu ...	sky
277. ubara ...		cididu	glow (spark)
	,,	cidinu, rimutu, nira-rutu	protection (law), grace, help
278. asilal ...		risātu ...	eldest (first)
279. bat		dūru, mitutu ...	fortress, death
280. dadhru ...		dabibu ...	deviser
281. mermer ...		Rammanu	the air-god (Rimmon)
282. lū		dalakhu ...	to trouble
guk... ...	,,	cuccu ...	?
283. gā, de ...		taru, nacaru, passakhu, napalu, nakamu, ecimu, cipupi, pala-khu, calalu, saba-dhu, nacru-sa-amati	to return, to change, to pass over, to throw down, to punish, to strip, ?, to worship, to complete, staff (?), breaker of faith
284. cus		nākhu, nikhu, tsalamu	to rest, rest, shadow (eclipse)
šur, sur ...	,,	iššu, saccagunū ...	mighty, ?
	,,	izzis, uzzis	strongly (?)
285. ra		rakhatsu, akhazu, ana, rapasu	to inundate, to take, to (for), to enlarge
sa ...	,,	lā, lū, ...	not, ?

Phonetic Value (Accadian word).	Cuneiform Character.	Assyrian rendering.	Meaning.
285. kal (?) ...		cipru ...	region (race)
286. uśan ...		? ...	?
286a. ?	(in Pers. Insc.)	napalcutu	rebel
287. sa, gum, cū, mulu, lugur, nita		nisu, avilu ...	man, man
287a. azalak ...		azlacu ...	?
287b. dinik ...		sibtsu ...	?
288. sis ... ... ur (uru) ...		akhu, urinnu ... natsaru, nuru ...	brother, peacock to help, light
289. da [individualising affix in Acc.]		pidnu, nasū-sa-nisi ... pidhnu	field (furrow), top of a man yoke
290. zak (śak), zik		zaggu, amutu, cbiltu, adi, isaru, idu, itatu, pūlū, bircu, atsidu, isdu, bamatu, tsēru, emuku, asaridu, sumelu, ricśu, pādu	?, true (?), lordship, up to, just (straight), house, wall, cattle, knee, ?, heap, high place, supreme, deep, eldest, left hand, bond (building), frontier
tami ...	„		
zikkad ...	„	simtu ...	destiny
291. ma, mamū ...		sacanu, padinnu, mātu zacaru ...	to dwell, plain, country to commemorate
292. as		arratu, ciccinu, tsibutu, khasakhu, madadu	curse (enchantment), ?, wish, want, to measure
dessu ...	„	samu	heaven
293. gal, [tak in Susian.]		gallu, rabu ...	great, great
293a. utaccal ...		utaccilu ...	?
293b. ulad ...		dabikhu ...	?

Phonetic Value (Accadian word).	Cuneiform Character.	Assyrian rendering.	Meaning.
293c. kigal ...		muhirru ...	*ruler*
294. ?		karū... ...	*to invoke*
295. mir, ega ...		agu, banu, uzzu ...	*crown (halo), tiara, coronet*
dhun-gunū ...	„	śibbu, śibkhū, iltanu	*girdle, turban* (Heb. מטפחת), *north* (?)
296. bar (bara) ...		paraccu, basamu, udu, risku	*altar (sacrifice), balsam, aloe, nard*
sar (sara) ...	„	sāru, paraccu ...	*incense* (?), *altar*
297. bur, gul (?), ninda-gunū		isdu, būru, śalatu-sa-*, abnu	*heap, ?, ?, stone*
298. bis (pis), cu'a-gunū		cu'a-gunū, palakhu, rapadu, mamluv, khuzabu, salalti, napasu	*Merodach of the garden* (?), *to worship, ?, rain, clay* (?), *spoiling, to stretch*
kir (cir), gar	„	cabattu ...	*liver*
299. gar, kar ...		abbuttu, karru ...	*?, ?*
300. pir		?	?
301. id		idu, ikhitu, cuśśu ...	*hand (power), one* (fem.), *throne* [the character seems originally to have denoted a comb]
a	„	karnu	*horn*
302. ?		paratsu ...	*to speak falsely*
303. uru, muru ...		gablu	*the middle (battle)*
unu ...	„	nasacu, niku, subtu, biru	*to pour out, libation, seat,* ?
304. de		saku - sa - ikli, sicitu, tupuku, nas'u	*top of a field, surface* (?), *district, to tear up (remove)*
śi, idgal ...	„	nappakhu	*to dawn*
umun ...	„	mummu	?
ubil ...	„	sagumu	?

Phonetic Value (Acca-dian word).	Cuneiform Character.	Assyrian rendering.	Meaning.
305. ? ...		?	" *hermaphrodite* " (Oppert)
306. lil		lillu	*sorcery* (?)
307. śukh, lukh ...		tsabatu, ri'u, tallicu ...	*to seize, shepherd, a march*
308. ? ...		pulu... ...	*cattle*
309. alam, alala, bi-seba		tsalamu ...	*image*
lani, sabaru	,,	bunnu ...	*image (sculpture)*
310. bisebi ...		samsu	*the sun*
311. khilip ...		ilu	*god*
312. ?		belatu	*lady*
313. śik, śizi, ara...		arku, urcitu... ...	*green, verdure*
	,,	banu	*old gazelle*
314. dub... ...		napatsu, egu ...	*to break in pieces, to surround*
balag ...	,,	balangu	*division*
bamiś ...	,,		
315. sa		lu	?
nā	,,	pidhnu ...	*yoke*
316. accada, bur-bur		tilla, saki	*highland (Accad), the sum-mits*
317. su, sugab, kat		katu, idu, gimillu, emuku, ubanu	*hand, hand (power), benefit, hollow, peak*
317*a.* khul (?) ...		nigū, gamalu ...	*control* (?), *to benefit*
317*b.* tucundi ...		summa ...	*thus (if)*
318. curu ...		damiku ...	*prosperous*
(*See No.* 111.)			

Phonetic Value (Accadian word).	Cunciform Character.	Assyrian rendering.	Meaning.
319. sâ		damaku	*fortunate*
gisimmar ...	„	gisimmaru	?
320. lab, lul, ruk, nar, rar, pakh, lib		śarru ...	*king*
320. se		scum, ziru, ittu, amaru, magaru	*corn (grain), seed, wheat, wheat, happy*
niga ...	„	marû	*young*
sana, sananabacu	„	irbittu	*four*
		?	*hin (a measure)*
321. bu (pu), śir, gid		śēru, sadadu, ericu, nūru	*?, long, to extend, light*
sepuz ...	„	maru, naśakhu, rabadu, ebiru	*young, to remove, to adorn (?), to cross*
śus, guz ...	„	napakhu, Davcina ...	*to dawn, the goddess Daukê*
322. ? ...		? ...	?
323. sud		ericu, rukutu ...	*to extend, distant*
śu	„	śir-gunu	?
ezu	„	arû, zaraku, śulukhu, irisu, sakhalu	*?, bucket (?), pardon (?), request (?), plague (?)*
324. tsir (śir) ...		tsiru... ...	*serpent*
mus...	„	musu ...	*serpent (?)*
325. uz (uts, uś), śir		uśu, tsiru ...	*?, serpent*
326. tir ...		cisatu (kistu), dayanu,	*jungle, judge*
327. te, dimmenna		temennu, tsabatu, cuśśu	*floor (foundation-stone), to seize, throne*
te, dikh (of Ass. origin)	„	dakhu ...	*to face*
327a. mulla ...		? ...	? .
327b. unu, temencs-gunū		maca *	*

Phonetic Value (Accadian word).	Cuneiform Character.	Assyrian rendering.	Meaning.
328. car	☵𐏉	caru, ediru, ecimu, dakhu	*fortress, to arrange, to strip, to face*
329. u ... ... pur, bur ... ge ... ... umun ...	𒀸 " " "	belu, śaru, ubanu, śilu esritu, suplu ... mikhiltu ... ... damu	*lord, king, peak, rock* *ten, below* *battle* *blood (offspring)*
330. babar ...	⟨𐏐	putstsū-sa-kan-dubba	*white surface to receive an inscription*
331. si, lim (liv, li) ir (?), tim (?)	⟨𐏐- " " "	enu, amaru, makharu panu, igu ... ... mātu, ecitsu ...	*eye, to see, before (witness)* *presence (face),* ? *country,* ?
332. khul ...	⟨𐏐-𒌅-𒄑	kullulu, limuttu, khumkhum	*accursed (evil), baneful, sultry*
333. curuv ...	⟨𐏐-𒉺𐏐	pakadu, damku ...	*overseer, propitious (of good omen)*
334. seba, izcu (?)	⟨𐏐-𒈨-𒈨𐏉	tugultu, ardutu, libittu	*service, servitude, omen*
335. ?	⟨𐏐-𒈨𐏉	?	*(astronomical) observation*
336. pam (pav, pā)	⟨𐏐- 𒀸𐏉	zacaru, nabu, tamatu, namru, utu	*to remember, to proclaim,* ?, *bright,* ?
337. ar	⟨𐏐-𐏉⟨𐏐	?	?
338. ? ...	⟨𐏐- ⟨𐏐	nemicu ...	*deep wisdom*
339. va ... ... tsi	⟨𐏐-𒂍 "	u, naku, śarru ...	*and, to sacrifice, king*
340. timkhir ...	⟨𐏐-⟨𒂼⟨𐏐 ⟨𐏐-⟨𒂼⟨𐏐	Nabiuv ...	*the god Nebo*
341. pikh ...	⟨𐏐-𐏐⟨𐏐	?	?

Phonetic Value (Accadian word).	Cuneiform Character.	Assyrian rendering.	Meaning.
342. di, dim ...	[cuneiform]	dēnu (dīnu), salamu, śulmu, erisu, sana-nu, sakabu, śararu, casadu	to judge, to end, rest, to ask, to rival, to make speak, ?, to conquer
śa	,,	milcu, śarar-śirri ...	king (judge), ?
śilim, sallim (of Ass. origin)	,,	śulmu, sulummu ...	rest (completion, recompense), peace (alliance)
342a. śagar, śagalum	[cuneiform]	malicu ...	a king
343. ci (cina), cicū	[cuneiform]	itti (ittu), asru, kak-karu, mātu, irtsitu, saplu, asābu, anna, ema	with, place, ground, country, earth, lower, a dwelling, on, about
cizlukh ...	,,	mascanu ...	high place
343a. utu ...	[cuneiform]	citim-sa ...	below it (its lower part)
343b. canlab ...	[cuneiform]	suluv, nidutu, terictu, asru, ramanu	high, high place, extension, place, self
343c. siten ...	[cuneiform]	malacu ...	to rule
344. durud ...	[cuneiform]	carru	fortress
345. va (?), cicas (?)	[cuneiform]	sū	like (the same, ditto, repetition)
346. cusi... ...	[cuneiform]	? ...	?
347 sakkad ...	[cuneiform]	cubsu, Nabiuv ...	crown, the god Nebo
348. lit, lat (lad)...	[cuneiform]	?	?
ab	,,	arkhu ...	month
u	,,	... ...	...
349. cir (kir) ...	[cuneiform]	cīru, tsurru	plantation (?), bowels
ub	,,	ubbn	?
libis... ...	,,	labbu	heart (interior)
sem... ...	,,	khalkhallatu ...	desire (?)
350. metsi .	[cuneiform]	manzu ...	?

Phonetic Value (Accadian word).	Cuneiform Character.	Assyrian rendering.	Meaning.
351. ?		ditanu ...	*chamois* (?)
351*a*. alim, sagira-cu'a-igidu		Bilu, śarru, Beltu, mitanu, cuśariccu	*the god Bel, king, goddess Beltis, plague,* ?
352. cis (kis) ...		cissatu ...	*multitude*
353. ner		sepu...	*foot (basis)*
ne, pisim ...	"	emuku	*deep*
aric... ...	"	nēru, pisimmu ...	*yoke,* ?
	"	namru	*bright*
354. tidnu ...		akharru ...	*behind (the west)*
355. liliś		liliśu... ...	*barrier* (?)
356. zigarū ...		samū	*heaven*
357. sacan (?) ...		sacanu	*to appoint*
357. sadugacunu		na'idu,'ublu, nakhagun-matu, parsu'hu, śaśu, mūnu, selibbū	*insect* (?), *worm,* ?, *flea, moth, worm, worm*
dūgu ...	"	bircu, dābu, rikhu ...	*knee, good, odour* (or *breath*)
358. gingir ...		Istar ...	*the goddess Istar*
359. amar ...		buru, gannu... ...	*light* (?), *enclosure*
zur (*of Ass. origin*)	"	... ...	... ...
360. sigisse ...		niku, taslu, ciribu ...	*victim, prayer, offering*
361. nim, num, nū		saku, elamu, zibu ...	*top, highland (Elam), wolf*
enum (enuv)	"	samū	*heaven*
	"	nakaru - sa - semiri, garru, zumbu	*cutting by means of the diamond,* ?, *a fly*
362. zum		napalu ...	*to destroy*

Phonetic Value (Accadian word).	Cuneiform Character.	Assyrian rendering.	Meaning.
363. tum... ...		babalu ...	to bring down (produce)
364. lam (lav) ...		lammu ...	a seat (?)
365. nū		rabatsu ...	to rest
366. nā		udhalu (utalu) ...	eclipse (setting)
gud ...		rabatsu, nadu, mayalu	to lie down, to settle, bed
367. ul, dū, udbu-guddhu		cacabu ...	star
ru	„	clipu-sa-etsi, śumu, surru, calulu, taccabu, muttacbu	ship of wood, ?, ?, ?, point* (?), pointer (?)
368. cir (kir) ...		śalkhu (?)	citadel
369. bam, ban, bav		mitpanu, kastu ...	bow, bow
370. dim, sitimmu		cima, summa, banu, episu, basū, samadhu, matsū	like, thus, to form, to make, to be, ?, to find
tum (tuv)	„	banu, kharatsu, khartsu	to produce, to create, obscurity
cim, gim (of Ass. origin)	„	...	...
	„	idinnu ...	?
371. sita		ricśu, patlulu ...	bond, mixed (?)
372. * ruv ...		cirū	?
373. ...		?	?
374. mi, vi, gig, cu		tsalmu, cribu ...	shade (black), sunset
ge	„	musu	night
cuga ...	„		
375. śun		nardapu	pursuit (?)
gul (kul) ...	„	abatu	to destroy
	„	subtu, calu-sa-avili ...	seat, whole of a man

Phonetic Value (Accadian word).	Cuneiform Character.	Assyrian rendering.	Meaning.
376. dugud ... cab (Ass. value)		cabdu, miktu ...	*heavy (much, honor),* ?
377. gig ...		martsu, śimmu, cibtu	*sick, plague, affliction*
378. din (tin) ... gal		baladhu ... bitu	*life (family)* *house*
379. ugun ...		akhzētu, Naná ...	*?, the goddess Nana*
380. mukh ...		mukhkhu, eli, banu, alidu	*over, over, to create, to beget*
381. caccul ...		kakkullu, namzitu ...	*?, ?*
382. man, in, nis buśur ... śar (Ass. value)		śaru ... ... samsu, esrā	*king* *the sun, twenty*
383. cus (cusu) ...		pulu...	*cattle*
384. es ... ... esseb ... śin (Ass. value)		bitu ... ... salasā, Śinu ...	*house* *thirty, the Moon*
385. sanabi ...		irbahā	*forty*
386. usu		erib-samsi	*sunset*
387. nigin ...		cummu	*the interior of the earth*
388. lagar ...		lagaru	*?*
389. cizlukh (?) ...		mascanu ...	*high*
390. tul (dhul) ...		bakhilu, ridu-sa-riduti, sadu	*?, harem, hill*
dul		catamu	*to conceal*
mul... ...		mulu	*?*
durud ...		carru	*fortress*

Phonetic Value (Accadian word).	Cuneiform Character.	Assyrian rendering.	Meaning.
391. cû	𒑥	ellu, caśpu	*high (noble, precious), silver (money)*
391a. babbar ...	𒑥	caśpu	*silver*
391b. guski ...	𒑥	khuratsu	*gold*
392. mun ...	𒑥	idlû	*a hero*
393. dun... ... sul	 "	idlu, dannu ... ... śulum	*hero, strong* ?
394. eśa, śa ...	𒑥	khamesserit, Istar, imnu	*fifteen, the goddess Istar, right hand*
395. pad (pat), kur (?) ... suk	 "	śimtu, sipartu ...	*plague, bill (account)*
396. gam (gû) ... lus, gur ...	𒆖	iśacu, lanu, kan- duppi, musacnis, cubuśu, kabu	*to pour (?), a dwelling, a papyrus-scroll, subduer, a trampling, to speak*
397. * ...		*Sign of a division*	*between words or sentences*
398. * ...		*do. ; also a*	*contracted form of the number* 9
399. cur (kur) ... mat (mad) ... lat (lad), nat (nad), sat (sad) ra'er ...	 " " "	curu, sadu, elu, garu, nacaru, napakhu mâtu, casadu ... mâtu, sadu	*land, mountain (the east), high, foreign, hostile, to dawn* *country, to conquer (acquire)* *country, mountain*
400. ana			*to root-up*
401. lis, dil (dul)	𒀸	iddu * *	?

Phonetic Value (Accadian word.)	Cuneiform Character.	Assyrian rendering.	Meaning.
402. ud (utu, ut), par		samsu, yumu, namaru, enu, nahru-sa-yumi, urru, pitsu, atsu	*sun, day, to see, eye, dawning of day, light, white, to rise*
lakh... ...	"	samsu, śarru, ellu ...	*sun, king, high*
zal (śal), tam	"	samsu	*the sun*
sam (,u) ...	"	yumu, immu, samsu	*the day, the day, the sun*
zab, erim ...	"	tsābu, bibu	*soldier (host)*
babar ...	"	tsit-samsi, namaru ...	*sunrise, to see*
402a. e		atsu, makhkhu, padu	*to rise (issue), mighty, sceptre*
402b. ukh (ukhu) (see 405)		cusu, ruhtu... ...	*?, poison (?)*
402c. zabar ...		śiparru ...	*copper (bronze)*
403. bir		nuru, namaru ...	*light, to see*
erim, lakh ...	"	tsabbu	*soldier (host)*
zab, śab (Ass. values)			
403a. ◊ ❋ nus ...		pilu	*choice*
404. ? ...		niraru ...	*helper*
405. ukh... ...		ruhtu	*poison (philtre)*
406. pi		uznu	*ear*
ā, tal, pi, me	"	me, giltanu	*water, drop*
407. 'ā, āh ...		giltanu	*drop of water*
408. sā, lib, śini ...		labbu ...	*heart (middle, within)*
408a. śini ...		kunkut [or kuntar] ...	?
409. pis		eru, aladu	*pregnant, begetting*
410. bir		saradhu ...	*paint (?)*
411. nanam ...		cinu	*established (firm)*

4 *

Phonetic Value (Accadian word).	Cuneiform Character.	Assyrian rendering.	Meaning.
412. gudu ...	𒍣	?	*to set (end)*
413. zib (śib, tsib)	𒊸	zibbu ...	?
414. khi, khig ... dhi, khā ... id, sar (śarrab), śib (zib), dhum dar, dhar ... sar, dūgu (*See No.* 357)	(*also written*) " " " "	dhābu, cissatu, esiru cissatu-sa-same, bircu ... ... pallilu, Assuru ... cissatu, mādu, rabu, mukhudu, sutabū, dussu, nukhsu, pumalu, nakhasu-sanukhsi	*good, multitude, propitious (holy)* *legions of heaven, a knee* *a measure* *to mingle, the god Assur* *multitude, much, great, great,* ?, ?, *prosperity, powerful, prosperer of prosperity*
415. im ... .. sar ... ... mir, muru ... im ... ... imi	" " :, "	rukhu, rikhu, ramanu, palakhu, rarubatu sāru, samu ... ... nahdu, irbu, Rammanu pulukhtu, emuku, zumru samu, irtsitu, akhu, didu, sāru, zunnu, duppu	*wind (air, tempest, cardinal point), breath, self, to worship, fear* *brightness (sky), heaven* *bright, rain, the Air-god* *fear, deep, body (person)* *sky, earth, brother (?), ?, brightness, rain, tablet (?)*
415a. latakh ...	𒅎𒁁	uduntu-sa-rukhi ...	*quantity of wind*
416. kam (cam), kham	𒄠	... ...	*denotes ordinal numbers*
416a. esses ...	𒄠 𒌍	?	?
417. ah (h, hi) ...	𒄴, 𒀀 (*in Persian inscriptions*)	'umunu	*small worm*

Phonetic Value (Accadian word).	Cuneiform Character.	Assyrian rendering.	Meaning.
418. akh, ikh, ukh, (ukhu)		uplu, kalmatu, pursu'u, umunu	*worm, vermin, flea, small worm*
	„	rukhuku	*distant*
lammubi ...	„	nāpu	*worm*
419. bir		sapikhu ...	*a destroyer*
420. khar ...		semiru, esiru ...	*diamond, bracelet*
mur, ur, cin, kham	„	cirbu, khasu, zumru	*centre, liver, body*
420a. urus (= *the god Bel in Cassite*)		tirtu, tirtu-sa-khasē ...	*body (form),* ?
421. khus (khuś)		khussu	*beaten out (small gazelle)*
rus	„	russu	*young gazelle, blue cloth*
422. śukh, śukhar		cimmatu ...	*family (household)*
423. zun		mahdutu ...	*many*
424. ?		belatu ...	*lady*
425. ? ...		rabu, dannu ...	*great, strong*
426. zicara ...		samu ...	*the sky*
427. dis (tis), gi ... ana (*Ass. value*)		ana, śarru, estinu ...	*to, king, one*
	„		
428. lal		malu, madhu, sapacu, sakalu, ubburu-sa-amati, khizu, sapalu, etsilu, śaradu-sa-cipratu, śanaku, cima, tartsu, callu, ensu	*to fill, to fall (?), to pour out, to weigh (pay), crossing of the sea, ?, under (below), idle (?), ?, chain, like, facing (in the time of), to restrain, sick*
nas, lū ...	„	sakalu, tsabatu, tsimdu, nīru, aniru	*to weigh, to seize, yoke, yoke, yoke*
429. lal, ū ...		sukalulu ...	*to equal (reach)*

Phonetic Value (Accadian word).	Cuneiform Character.	Assyrian rendering.	Meaning.
430. usar... ...		settu	*bank*
431. ucu		labnu ...	*brick*
432. nanga ...		nagu (*of Acc. origin*)	*a district*
433. lalu... ...		libbātu ...	*brickwork*
434. me		kulu, kālu, tamtsu, zicaru, takhatsu, dūtu, meh, samu	*assembly, to assemble, mass, man, battle,* ?, *100, sky, sign of the plural*
isip, sib (sip)	„	ramcu	*herd*
435. mes (mis) ...		mahdutu, libbu ...	*many, heart,* sign of the plural
436. kas, ili ...		sinu, sanu	*two, repetition (ditto)*
min... ...	„		
437. 'a (*forms participles in Acc.*)	(*also written*)	me, abu, 'ablu ...	*water, father, son*
pur	„	nahru	*river*
dur	„	labacu	?
it	„	nāku	*pure (sacrifice)*
ga, e ...	„	rakipu	?
437*a*. eba ...		melu	*flood*
437*b*. ara... ...		milcu ...	*king* (or *crocodile*)
437*c*. ir		dimtu, calū naccalu, unninnu	*a pile, complete vessel,* ?
437*d*. aria ...		nahru ...	*river*
438. ai		abu	*father*
439. ? ...		iddu...	*bitumen*
440. kumun ...		Tasmitu	*the goddess Tasmit* (wife of Nebo)
441. za (tsa) ...		arbu, ci, atta ...	*four, like, thou*

Phonetic Value (Accadian word).	Cuneiform Character.	Assyrian rendering.	Meaning.
441a. uknu ...	𒀹	ibbu... ...	*white*
442. kha		nunu, ranu, simru, nabu, khalaku	*fish, ?, ?, to proclaim, to divide (destroy)*
'a, ua ...	,,	Cû'a... ...	*Merodach's oracle*
443. gug (guk) ...		śamtu ...	*blue*
444. zakh ...		?	?
444. ner ...		nēr	*measure or space of six hundred*
445. dar, ara ...		?	80
446. essa... ...		salsatu ...	*three*
446a. gar or sā ...		ribu	*a fathom*
446b. gi (?) ...		kanu... ...	*a cane (measure)*
447. sana, sa ... irba (Ass. value)		irbu, ribu, nitu ...	*four, a quarter, ?*
gar	,,	episu, sacanu, saracu, girū, naśakhu-satirti, rakhatsu, zaltu, nūru, khamdhu, gamalu, maśakhu, garru, sēmu, nitu, acalu, cumuru, sucunnu, eristu	*to make (do), to dwell, to furnish, hostile, removal of body, to inundate, battle, light, speedy, to benefit, removal, food, obedient, ?, food, ?, fortress, bride (?)*
sā	,,	?, mala, nasu ...	*a measure (a quart), as many as, to lift up*
448. śa, para ...		khamsa	*five*
ya, i ...	,,	nahdu	*glorious*
449. as		sissu ...	*six*
450. sisna ...		śibu	*seven*
451. ? ...		tisu	*nine*

Phonetic Value (Accadian word).	Cuneiform Character.	Assyrian rendering.	Meaning.
452. nin		allatu	*wife*
453. ? ...		sumelu ...	*the left hand*
454. esseb ...		sarru ...	*king*
455. duk, tuc (tug) dū		tucu, isu, akhazu, si-mū, zarakhu, tsa-maru	*to have, to have, to possess, to place, to rise, to rise* (of stars)
456. ur		khamamu, etsidu, na-raru, aruru, khazu	*heat (celestial sphere), to hew (?), to burn, burnt,* ?
457. sussana ...		sussanu ...	*one-third*
457a. gigim ...		ecimmu ...	*demon*
458. sanibi ...		sinibu	*two-thirds (forty)*
459. utuk ...		uduccu	*spirit*
460. kiguśili, parap		parapu ...	*five-sixths*
461. mascim ...		maṣcimmu	*a demon*
462. cu	,	usibu, subtu, marcaśu, ina, ana, rubū, akru, tucultu	*to sit down, seat, bondage, in, to, prince, precious, service*
iputugulacu	"		
dur, pī, tul ...	"	tucultu, nukhu, zacaru	*service, rest, to record*
us	"	dhemu	*law*
zi	"	cemu	*clothes*
tū	"	nadu, tsubatu ...	*to place, clothes*
sc	"	tucullu	*trust (service)*
tus (dus), khun, seba, mugu, ipu-tugulacu			
	"	nasu-sa-eni, muśaru, dū, tsillu, mulū, succu, sa-subat-apzi	*raising of the eyes, inscription, ?, side, ascent (?), booth, seat of the underworld*

Phonetic Value (Accadian word).	Cuneiform Character.	Assyrian rendering.	Meaning.
463. gil, khap (khab), gur (gu), cir, (kir, gir), rim, girim, gar, zam, mik, lagab		lagabu	?
	„	racaśu, pukhkhuru, gararu-sa-nisi, śecuru, dubutu, bahalu, bihisu	to bind, gathering, tumult of men, enclosing, ?, to fear (?), ?
463a. puda (gidda)		aricu, ruku	long, distant
464. zar (tsar, śar)		?	?
465. umuna ...		alapu	a thousand "festival" (Lenormant)
466. zarip ...		?	?
467. uh, ua ...		rubtsu, cabasu, pikannu	flock, sheep
468. ? ...		taccabu	?
469. suk ... ... umun ...	„	tsutsu ... ... khammu	aquatic plant (plant, marsh) heat (zone)
470. pu ... ... pur (See No. 223)	„	tsutsu ... ... pūru, muspalu ...	pool (marsh) pool (?), low ground
471. bul		?	?
472. ? ...		?	a cornfield (?)
473. ? ...		?	?
474. cu (?) or sāgar (?)		khusukhkhu ...	famine

Phonetic Value (Accadian word).	Cuneiform Character.	Assyrian rendering.	Meaning.
475. sü	𒀸	zirku ...	*a bucket*
476. gur	𒀸	apśu... ...	*running water*
zicuv ...	,,	samū ...	*heaven*
477. ? ...	𒀸	? ...	?
478. ? ...	𒀸	iddu (*see No.* 439) ...	*bitumen*
479. ? ...	𒀸	narcabtu ...	*chariot*
480. ? ...	𒀸	pagru ...	*corpse*
481. nigin ...	𒀸 (*See No.* 463)	napkharu, pakharu, śakharu, nagarruru, tsai'idu, tsadu-sa-lavē, pasaru, epusu, racaśu	*collection, to collect, to sur-round, tumultuous as-sembly, hunter, hunter of the neighbourhood, to ex-plain, to make, to bind*
ilammi ...	,,		
481a. cilidagal ...	𒀸 𒀸	? ...	*library*
482. ? ...	𒀸	* ...	*such an one (so and so)* ·
483. ip (ib, ibbi)...	𒀸	banu, ligittu, tupuktu	*to create, log* (measure), *race*
dar	,,	nibittu, gisru ...	*name, strong*
daruv ...	,,	izkhu	?
uras... ...	,,	sa-issik-icribi, baru, ramcu, urasu, acmu, ligittu, nibittu	*who hears prayers, ?, a herd, ?, log, name*
484. lu	𒀸, 𒀸	tsini, cirru	*flocks, sheep*
dib (dip) ...	,,	dibbu, lavu, ctiku, tsabatu, titsbatu, tamkhu	*tablet, tablet, to cross, to seize, seizure, hold*
udu, dū ...	,,	inmiru, dassu ...	*lamb, gazelle*
u, sib (sip) ...	,,		
guccal ...	,,	guccallu	?
	,,	cavu, bahu, garru ...	*to burn* (?), *chaos, food*

Phonetic Value (Accadian word).	Cuneiform Character.	Assyrian rendering.	Meaning.
485. ki, kin (cin)	𒌋, 𒌋, 𒌋	turtu, sipru, pāru, sitehu, senikhu, amaru	*dove*(?), *writing* (*explanation*), ?, ?, ?, *messenger*
486. sak, sik ... śik, ukh ... mut (?) ...	𒌋 ,, ,,	saradu .. ... supātu, sipatu ...	*paint* *cloth, stuff*
487. ? ...	𒌋, 𒌋		*plank*
488. sis ... ... busus (*Ass. value*)	𒌋 ,,	pasāsu ... damamu ...	*to extend* (?) *to perish*
489. ? ...	𒌋	tur-sipri ...	*librarian* (*scribe*)
490. dar (dara) ...	𒌋	dahmu ...	?
491. munsub ...	𒌋	khir-tū ...	?
492. gur	𒌋	carū	?
493. erin	𒌋	erinu ...	*cedar* (?)
494. lig (lik) ... tas (das) ... lis ... ... ur (*Ass. value*)	𒌋 ,, ,, ,,	calbu, pultu, baltu, uru nisu (?), nacaru ... nesu ...	*dog*, ?, ?, *lion* *man, enemy* *lion*
495. dhu ... ... al	𒌋 ,,	cibu, alacu ... ... pāsu, apasu, sundu, ruedu	*mass* (*body, weight*), *to go* ?, ?, ?, ?
496. śal, rak ... kal (gal), murub mak, muk ...	𒌋, 𒌋 ,, ,,	nestu, uru ... ... uru ... ... muccu ...	*a woman, a city* *a city* *a building*
496a. murub ...	𒌋	uru	*a city*
496b. murub ...	𒌋	pū, uśukhu	*mouth*, ?

Phonetic Value (Accadian word).	Cuneiform Character.	Assyrian rendering.	Meaning.
497. gar	𒀳	nan * ⊛	?
498. nin, ni, mak...	𒀭, 𒀯	beltu, rubatu ...	*lady, princess*
499. dam (dav) ...	𒁮, 𒁯	assatu, allatu, [mutu]	*woman, wife, [husband]*
500. gu	𒄖	kā, ilu-sa-napkhari, mātu, pānu	?, *god of the world, land, face*
501. ? ...	𒄔	?	... ?
502. tsu, tsum, rak, ri, khal (khil)	𒋢	?	... ?
503. nik (nig) ...	𒐑	?	... ?
504. i ...	𒄿	?	... ?
505. el (il) ... (*See No.* 211)	𒂖 "	śikhapcu, ellu, bibu teliltu	?, *high* (?), ? *hymn*
506. lum, khum ...	𒈝	unnubu ...	?
507. mun, mur, ucu	𒈬	labinu, libittu, malgu, Śivannu	*brick, brickwork, brick, the month Sivan*
508. ? ...	𒊓	ussusu ...	*foundation*
509. su, mastenu	𒁹	baru, cribu, nikhappu, lēmu, śakhpu, asaru, śikhu, caramu, adaru, khīsu, cissatu	?, *to set*, ?, ?, *overthrow, a place* (?), *plague, a vineyard* (?), *darkness* (?), ?, *multitude*
essā... ...	"	scpu...	*a foot*
su	,,	mastenu ...	*mischief*
dhiv, sumasdin	,,		
	,,	essutu ...	*change* (*time*)
510. śik (sik, sig)	𒈫	siktu, matsu, mātu, ensu, nadkhu, śakhpu	?, *to find* (?), *country, sick, fragment, overthrow*
510a. ?	𒐖	? ...	"*a sixtieth*" (Oppert)

Phonetic Value (Accadian word).	Cuneiform Character.	Assyrian rendering.	Meaning.
511. ris	III ⟨Y⟨	khumtsiru	?
cis	,,	pešu... ...	?
* mis ...	,,	citstu ...	jungle
512. ? ...		pulukhtu ...	fear (worship)
513. gibil ...		kilutu	a burning
cibir ...	,,	sarapu, makiddu ...	to burn, a burning
514. en		siptu ...	lip (paragraph, incantation)
515. isi, šulsa, su-khul			?,
sukhub ...	,,	šūppatu ...	
516. sutul, sudun		nîru	yoke
517. ? ...		isatu... ...	fire
518. khul ...		khidutu	sin
ucus ...	,,	cissu, padu	multitude, ?
bibra ...	,,	bibru, nigu	joy (?), authority
519. dhul ...		? ...	?
520. šik		? ...	?
521. sikka ...		atudu ...	he-goat
522. ? ...		? ...	?

N.B.—A Star (*) signifies that one or more characters have been lost by a fracture of the tablet. *Khi*, a value of No. 180, has been accidentally omitted.

The following is a list of the characters which express the open or simple syllables of the Assyrian alphabet. The beginner is advised to commit it to memory before advancing further in the study of the language. The letters of the Hebrew alphabet are added in order to explain the transliteration adopted for Assyrian sounds.

א, *a, â, ha* 𒀀

ב, *b.*
פ, *p.*
} ab, ib, ub.
{ ba, bi, bu, be.
pa, pi, or pu.

ג, *g.*
ך, *c.*
ק, *k.*
} ag, ig, ug.
{ ga, gi, gu, ge.
ca, ci, cu.
ka, ki, ku.

ד, *d.*
ט, *dh.*
ת, *t.*
} ad, id, ud.
{ da, di, du, de.
dha, or dhi, dhu, dhe.
ta, ti, tu, te.

ה, *h.* ah, hi, h, uh.

ו, *u, v.* hu, û, u, va, u. *See also* m.

ז, *z.*
ס, *s.*
צ, *ts.*
} az, iz, uz.
{ za, zi, zu.
śa, śi, śu.
tsa, tsi, tsu.

ח, *kh.* akh, ikh *and* ukh, ukh; kha, khi, khu.

י, *i.* i, 'i.

ל, *l.* al, il, ul, el; la, li, or lu.

☐, *m*, also *v.* ⟨ₐₘ/ₐᵥ⟩ am,av, ⟨ᵢₘ/ᵢᵥ⟩ im,iv, ⟨ᵤₘ/ᵤᵥ⟩ um;uv; ▷ᛁ *or* ▷ᛁᛁᛁ ⟨ₘₐ/ᵥₐ⟩ ma,va, ⟨ₘᵢ/ᵥᵢ⟩ mi,vi, ⟨ₙᵤ/ᵥᵤ⟩ nu,vu, ▷ ⟨ₘₑ/ᵥₑ⟩ me,ve.

], *n.*	⊢┿ an, ⊨∰ *or* ⟪⊨∰ in, ⊣⊀ᛁ na, ⊠⊞ ni, ⊁ nu, ⊠◁⊣ᛁ ne.	
	⊨ᛁᛁᛁ un, ⊢ᛁ en.	

𝒴, *e.* ⊨ᛁᛁ.

⟍, *r.*	⟨ᛁ⊢⊢ᛁᛁ⟨ ar, ⊠∰ ir, ⊑⊒ᛁᛁ *or* ᛁ⊣ ur.	⊨⊢ᛁᛁ ra, ⊢ᛁᛁ⟨ ri, ◁ᛁᛁᛁ *or* ⟨ᛁᛁ ru.

𝓌, *s.*	⊢ *or* ⊨ as, ⊠⊀ᛁᛁ is, ⊠⊣ᛁ us, ⟪⟨ es.	⩔ *or* ⊨⊀ᛁᛁ sa, ⟨ᛁ⊢ si, ⊨ᛁ *or*] su, ⊁ *or* ⊨⊨ᛁ se.

Diphthongs :— ᛁᛁ ᛁᛁ ai (*aya*), ⊑⊨ᛁᛁ ya (*ia*).

An ideograph is often indicated by a *phonetic complement* which gives the first or last syllable of the Assyrian word which is to be read. Thus ⊁ ⊀ᛁ is to be rendered by some part (according to the context) of the aorist *acsud* " I acquired."

Three main rules to be observed in selecting the value of a character are (1) that that power is to be chosen, the first or last consonant of which is the same as the consonant which ends the preceding syllable or begins the next; (2) that no Assyrian word, as a general rule, ought to contain more than three radical letters; and (3) that values consisting only of a consonant and a vowel are to be preferred to those in which the vowel is enclosed between two consonants.

An open syllable (that is, one which begins with a vowel) only exceptionally follows a character which terminates in a consonant; and all words end with the line. Determinative Prefixes (D.P.) are a great assistance to the reader. These are unpronounced ideographs which are always set before certain classes of persons and objects; so that their presence enables us to tell with certainty the nature of the following word. There are also Determinative Affixes (D.A.) which serve the same purpose.

The determinative prefixes and affixes are as follows:

PREFIXES:—

►►𝌆 (*'ilu*)	denotes	a god or goddess.
𝌆 or 𝌆	,,	a man.
𝌆	,,	a woman.
►𝌆 or ►𝌆 (*âlu*)	,,	a city or town.
𝌆 (*matu*)	,,	a country.
𝌆 (*nahru*)	,,	a river.
𝌆 or 𝌆 (*bîtu*)	,,	a house.
𝌆 (*rukhu*)	,,	wind, or point of the compass.
𝌆 (*tulu*)	,,	a mound.
𝌆 (*abnu*)	,,	a stone.
𝌆 (*illu*)	,,	a metal.
𝌆 (*etsu*)	,,	tree or wood.

PREFIXES:—

►𝌆 (*kanu*)	denotes	grass, reeds, &c.
𝌆 (*'imiru*)	,,	animal.
►𝌆 (*itstsuru*)	,,	a bird.
𝌆	,,	an insect.
𝌆	,,	an official or class of persons.
►𝌆 (*bilu*)	,,	a ruler.
𝌆 (*seru*)	,,	a limb or body.
►𝌆 or 𝌆 (*arkhu*)	,,	a month.
𝌆 (*lubustu*)	,,	clothing.
𝌆 (*cacabu*) or 𝌆	,,	a star.

AFFIXES:—

𝌆	denotes	the plural.
𝌆	,,	the dual.
𝌆	,,	an ordinal number.

AFFIXES:—

𝌆 (*irtsitu*)	denotes	a place.
►𝌆 (*itstsuru*)	,,	a bird.

THE NOUNS.

Nouns substantive and adjective do not differ in form in Assyrian.

The adjective always follows its substantive, and has neither comparative nor superlative.

Nouns are of two genders, masculine and feminine, and abstract nouns take the feminine form. Many words are both masculine and feminine, and may take the terminations of both genders.

There are two numbers, singular and plural; and a dual is found in the case of those nouns which denote doubles, like "the eyes." Adjectives as well as substantives admit the dual form.

There are three cases, the nominative, ending in -*u;* the genitive, ending in -*i;* and the accusative, ending in -*a;* but great laxity prevails in the use of these forms.

The case-terminations have a final *m* (or *v*), termed the *mimmation.* This was usually dropped in the later Assyrian inscriptions, though the Babylonian dialect preserved it to the last.

When one substantive governs another, the governing noun loses the case-endings (and mimmation), and the governed noun which immediately follows commonly assumes the termination of the genitive. Thus *bil* is "lord," but *bil nuri,* "lord of light."

The feminine singular changes the *u* of the nominative masculine into -*ūtu,* -*ătu,* and -*ĭtu* (or *ĕtu*). The last two forms (*ătu* and *ĭtu*) might elide the vowel, unless the root is a "surd" one, like *sar,* when the final letter is doubled, producing *sarrătu,* "queen." In the plural the feminine ending became -*ātu* and -*ītu* or -*ĕtu.*

The oldest form of the plural masculine was in -*ānu,* which was originally used for both genders. We also find traces of a reduplicated plural, like *māmi,* "waters," and of a plural in -*ūnu,* like *dilūnu,* "buckets." Another form of the plural masculine was in -*ūtu* (carefully to be distinguished from the feminine singular in -*ūtu*). This is the form of the masculine plural adopted by all adjectives. The most common termination of the masculine plural was in -*e* or -*i.* These plurals are in many cases indistinguishable from the genitive case of the singular. The ending of the dual was *ā.*

There is a curious plural in -*tan,* which combines the feminine and masculine terminations. It expresses a *collection* of anything, e.g., *e-bir-tā-an,* "a ford."

PARADIGMS OF NOUNS.

The Characters to be transliterated by the Student.			The Characters to be added Student.	
Masculines :—				
Sing. Nom. ...	𒈬𒈨𒊒 (na - ci - ru)	*an enemy*	mu-śa-ru (*Nos.* 23, 116, 22).	*an in*
„ Gen. ...	𒈬𒈨𒊑		mu-śa-ri	
„ Acc. ...	𒈬𒈨𒊏		mu-śa-ra	
Plural	𒈬𒈨𒊑		mu-śa-rē *or* mu-śa-ri	
Sing. Construct. state	𒈬𒈨		mu-śar ... :..	
Sing. Nom. ...	𒈽𒄴𒇻 (na - akh - lu)	*a brook*	śar-ru (*Nos.* 193, 22)	*a*
„ Gen. ...	𒈽𒄴𒊑		śar-ri ...	
„ Acc. ...	𒈽𒄴𒊏		śar-ra ...	
Plural	𒈽𒊑		śar-ri	
Sing. Construct. state	𒈽		śar	
Sing. Nom. ...	𒍣𒊒 (zic - ru)	*record*	nac-lu (*Nos.* 57, 484)	*co*
„ Gen. ...	𒍣𒊑		nac-li ...	
„ Acc. ...	𒍣𒊏		nac-la ...	
Plural Nom. ...	𒍣𒇻𒌈		nac-lu-tu	
„ Gen. ...	𒍣𒇻𒋾		nac-lu-ti	

The Characters to be transliterated by the Student.			The Characters to be added by the Student.		
Masculines :—					
Construct. Sing.	 𒀯 𒂖	record	na-cal	...	complete
Construct. Pl....	 𒀹 𒐻 𒁹		nac-lu ut...	...	
Sing. Nom. ...	 𒄯𒋢	fortress	khar-su ...	...	a forest
„ Gen. ...	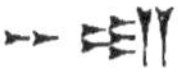 𒄯𒋛		khar-si	...	
„ Acc. ...	 𒄯 𒐀	... *	khar-sa ...	...	
Plural Nom. ...	𒄯 𒐊 [or 𒐊 𒐊]		khar-sä-nu [or khar-sa-a-nu]		
„ Gen. ...	𒄯 𒐊 𒋗		khar-sä-ni	...	
„ Acc. ...	𒄯 𒐊 𒈾		khar-sä-na	... ...	
Construct. Sing.	 𒐊 𒂖 𒅖		kha-ra-as...	... ...	
Construct. Pl....	𒄯 𒐊 𒈾		khar-sä-an	...	...
Feminines :—					
Sing. Nom. ...	 𒂊 𒇷 𒌈	a lady	'i-lä-tu	...	goddess
„ Gen. ...	𒂊 𒇷 𒋾	. ...	'i-lä-ti	...	
„ Acc. ...	𒂊 𒇷 �		'l-lä-ta	...	
Plural Nom. ...	𒂊 𒇷 𒐊 𒌈 [or 𒇷 𒌈]		'i-lä-a tu [or 'i-lä-tu]		
„ Gen. ...	 𒂊 𒇷 𒐊 𒋾 [or 𒀸]		'i-la-a·ti [or 'i-la-a-te]		
„ Acc. ...	 𒂊 𒇷 𒐊 𒌈		'i-la-a-ta ...	...	

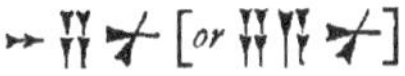

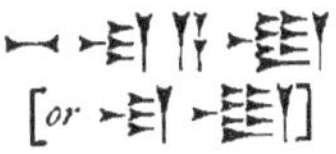

5*

The Characters to be transliterated by the Student.			The Characters to be added by the Student.	
Feminines :—				
Construct. Sing.	[cuneiform]	a lady	'l-lāt... ...	goddess
Construct. Pl.	[cuneiform]		'i-la-a-at	
Sing. Nom. ...	[cuneiform]		'il-tu ...	
„ Gen. ...	[cuneiform]		'il-ti	
„ Acc. ...	[cuneiform]		'il-ta ...	
Plural	*as before*		*as before*	
Sing. Nom. ...	[cuneiform]		'i-li-tu	
„ Gen. ...	[cuneiform]		'i-li-ti	
„ Acc. ...	[cuneiform]		'i-li-ta ...	
Plural Nom. ...	[cuneiform]		'i-li-e-tu ['ilētu] ...	
„ Gen. ...	[cuneiform] [*or* [cuneiform]]		'i-li-e-ti [*or* 'i-li-e-te]	...
„ Acc. ...	[cuneiform]		'i-li-e-ta	
Construct. Sing.	[cuneiform]		'i-lit	
Construct. Pl. ...	[cuneiform]		'i-lit	
Another Plural Noun	[cuneiform] *or* [cuneiform] &c., &c.		'i-li-i-tu ... ... *or* 'i-li-tu ... ... &c., &c.	

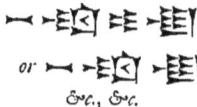

The Characters to be transliterated by the Student.			The Characters to be added by the Student.	
Feminines :—				
Sing. Nom. ...	 𒀊𒅖 𒌑 𒂼	tongue	'um-mu...	mother
„ Gen. ...	 𒀊𒅖 𒌑 𒈪		'um-mi	
„ Acc. ...	 𒀊𒅖 𒌑 𒈠		'um-ma...	
Plural Nom. ...	 𒀊𒅖 𒌑 𒈠𒀀𒌈		'um-ma-a-tu ['ummātu]	
„ Gen. ...	 𒀊𒅖 𒌑 𒈠𒀀𒋾		'um-ma-a-ti	
„ Acc. ...	 𒀊𒅖 𒌑 𒈠𒀀�		'um-ma-a-ta	
Construct. Sing.	 𒀊𒅖 𒌑 𒈠		'um ...	
Construct. Pl....	 𒀊𒅖 𒌑 𒈠𒀀𒀜		'um-ma-a-at	

Dual :—				
(Nom., Gen., Acc.)	 𒐊 𒁹𒐊 𒌋	the two hands	'uz-na-a ('uznā)	the two ears
	or  𒐊𒐊		se-pa-a (sepa) ...	the two feet

Nouns to be written in Assyrian characters, and declined :—

		Plural.
cu-du-du (*Nos.* 462, 212, 212)	*carbuncle*	(cu-du-de) (*Nos.* 462, 212, 342)
da-rum-mu (289, 11, 23) ...	*a dwelling* ...	(da-rum-mi *and* da-rum-me) (289, 11, 374 *or* 434)
ga-ru (227, 22) ...	*enemy*	(gari *and* ga-ri-e) (227, 83)
di-ku (342, 209) ...	*soldier*	(di-ku-tu) (342, 209, 60)
ci-su-du (343, 317, 212) ...	*captive*	(ci-su-du-tu) (343, 317, 212, 60)
dan-nu (241, 24) ...	*strong*	(dan-nu-tu) (241, 24, 60)
dup-pu (174, 321)	*tablet*	(dup-pa-a-nu) (174, 222, 437, 24)
e-mu-ku (239, 23, 209) ...	*deep power* ...	(e-mu-ka-a-nu) (239, 23, 20, 437, 24)

ri-su	*head*	(ri-sa-a-nu)
ci-sid-tu ...	*spoils*	(ci-si-da-a-tu)
i-sǎ-tu ...	*fire*	('i-sa-a-tu)
pul-khǎ-tu *or* pu-lukh-tu ...	*fear* ...	(pul-kha-a-tu)
cimmǎ-tu *or* cim-tu	*family* ...	(cim-ma-a-tu)
e-li-nĭ-tu	*high*	(e-li-nĕ-tu)
makh-ri-tu *or* ma-khir-tu	*former*	(makh-ra-a-tu)
gar-ru...	*expedition* ...	(gar-rĭ-tu *or* gar-ri-i-tu)
ag-gul-lu	*wagon*	(ag-gul-la-a-tu)
ap-pa-ru	*a marsh*	(ap-pa-ra-a-te)
ba-bu...	*a gate*	(ba-ba-a-tu)

THE NUMERALS.

The cardinals have two forms, masculine and feminine; but from 3 to 10 the feminine form is used for the masculine, and the masculine form for the feminine.

When the numerals are expressed in symbols 𝐘 signifies "one," 𝐘𝐘 "two," and so on. ⟨ stands for 10, ⟨𝐘 for 11, ⟨⟨ for 20, &c. 𝐘⊢ is 100, and ⟨𝐘⊢ (= 10 × 100) is 1000.

The cardinals are denoted by adding ◁◅ to the ordinal; thus 𝐘 ◁◅ is "first."

Sixty was the mathematical unit: the single wedge (𝐘) accordingly stands for the *soss*, or *sixty*, as well as for *one*. In fractions it is the understood denominator; thus, 𝐘𝐘𝐘 ⟨⟨⟨ (3.30) is 3 $\frac{30}{60}$, *i.e.* 3½.

TABLE OF CARDINAL AND ORDINAL NUMBERS.

			Masculine.		*Feminine.*		
1	=	𝐘	a-kha-du, e-du ...		i-khi-it ...		*First* = makh-ru, ris-ta-a-nu
	(*or* ⊱)		es-tin, cš-ta-a-nu ...		ikh-tu		
2	=	𝐘𝐘	sa-ni-e, sa-nu-'u, si-nu-'u		sa-ne-tu ...		*Second* = san-nu (*fem.* sa-nu-tu)
3	=	𝐘𝐘𝐘	sal-sa-tu ...		sal-su ...		*Third* = sal-sa-ai (*fem.* sa-li-is-tu)
4	=	𝐖	ir-bit-tu, ri-ba-a-tu ...		ar-ba-'i, ir-ba'i ...		*Fourth* = ri-bu
5	=	𝐖𝐘	kha-mis-tu, kha-mil-tu		kham-sa, kha-an-si ...		*Fifth* = kha-an-su
6	=	𝐘𝐘𝐘𝐘	si-sa-tu ...		sis-sa, sis-si ...		*Sixth* = [? sis-su]
7	=	𝐖𝐘𝐘	si-bit-tu, ši-bi-tu ...		ši-ba ...		*Seventh* = ši-bu-'u, ša-bi-tu
8	=	𝐖𝐘𝐘	[sam-na-tu] ...		sam-na		*Eighth* = [? šu-ma-nu]
9	=	𝐖𝐖	[ti-sit-tu] ...		[ti-is-'a] ...		*Ninth* = [ti-su-'u]
10	=	⟨	'e-sir-tu, 'es-e-rit, 'es-rit		'es-ru ...		*Tenth* = ['es-ru]
11	=	⟨𝐘	[estinesru ?] ...				

15	=	𒌋𒐌	kha-mis-se-rit
20	=	𒌋𒌋	es-ra-'a
30	=	𒌍	si-la-sa-'a
40	=	𒐏	ir-ba-'a, ir-ba-ya
50	=	𒐐	kha-an-sa-'a
60	=	𒁹	sus-su
70	=	𒁹𒌋	[si-bu-'a ?]
80	=	𒁹𒌋𒌋	?
90	=	𒁹𒌍	?
100	=	𒁹𒈨	me'
1000	=	𒐕𒈨	a-la-pu

EXAMPLE : 𒐎 𒐕𒈨 𒁹 𒁹𒈨 𒐐𒁹 ⸗𒌋 ⸗⸗⸗ = "2,451 oxen."

In writing "one" we sometimes find the phonetic complement added to the cipher to denote whether it has the masculine or the feminine form. Thus, 𒁹 ⸗𒐋 (EST-*en*) = *estin*, 𒁹 𒈨𒊩 (IKH-*it*) = *ikhit*.

Fractional numbers are as follows:— 𒂖 𒊩𒐌 𒀉 *su-un-nu* (ideographically written 𒀀) = "one-half," 𒁹 𒊩 𒀸 𒐊 𒀉 *su-us-sa-a-nu* = "one-third," 𒐕𒊩 𒊺 *si-ni-bu* = "two-thirds," 𒊹 𒂖𒐊 𒀀 *pa-ra-pu* = "five-sixths," 𒐐𒐌 𒀀 *ru-bu* = "one-fourth," ⸗𒐊 𒈬 *su-du* = "one-sixth," ⸗𒐊 𒂖 𒀉 *su-ma-nu* = "one-eighth," and 𒁹 𒈨𒊩 𒁹 *su-us-su* = "a sixtieth."

The adverbial numerals were formed by the termination *yānu*, as 𒊩 𒊺 𒂖𒐊 𒐊 𒀉 *sa-ni-e-'ā-nu*, or 𒊩 𒊺 𒂖𒐊 𒐊 𒀉 *sa-ni-ya-a-nu* "a second time" ("twice"), *sal-si-'a-nu* or *sal-si-ya-a-nu* "a third time." 𒊩 𒊺 𒈨𒂖 *sa-ni-tu* ("repetition") was used for "once," and in the later inscriptions it took the place of the adverbial numerals, e.g., *sa-ni-ti sal-sa* "the third time." *Sal-sa* is expressed in the Behistun inscription by the compound ideograph 𒍑.

Among the indefinite numerals may be reckoned ⸗𒌈 𒐊𒐊 *ca-lu*, ⸗𒌈 ⸗𒂖 *ca-la*, 𒂖𒐌 *cal*, ⸗𒀸 𒀀 *cul-lat* "all," 𒀀 𒀀 *gab-bu* "all," 𒄀𒐌 𒐐𒌋 *gim-ru* "the whole," 𒂖 𒈨𒐊 ⸗𒈨𒂖 *ma'-du-tu* "much," and ⸗𒌈 𒂖𒐌 ⸗𒈨𒂖 *ca-bit-tu* "much."

THE PRONOUNS.

THE PERSONAL PRONOUNS:—

1. *Sing.*	〔cuneiform〕 *or* 〔cuneiform〕	anacu... ...	= *I*
,,	〔cuneiform〕 〔cuneiform〕	yāti ... 〕 yātima ... 〕	= *I*
Plural ...	〔cuneiform〕	a-[nakh?]-ni	= *we*
2. *Sing. Masc.*...	〔cuneiform〕	atta	= *thou*
,, *Fem.* ...	〔cuneiform〕	atti	= *thou*
Com. Gend....	〔cuneiform〕 〔cuneiform〕	cātu ... ... 〕 cāta ... ... 〕	= *thou*
Plural, Masc....	〔cuneiform〕	attunu ...	= *you*
,, *Fem.* ...	〔cuneiform〕	[at-ti-na] ...	= *you*
3. *Sing. Masc.* ...	〔cuneiform〕 〔cuneiform〕	sū	= *he, it, him*
Fem. ...	〔cuneiform〕 〔cuneiform〕	sī	= *she, it, her*
Plural, Masc....	〔cuneiform〕 〔cuneiform〕 〔cuneiform〕 〔cuneiform〕 〔cuneiform〕	sūnu ... ... 〕 sun ... 〕 sunūtu ... 〕 sunūti ... 〕 sunūt ... ... 〕	= *they, them*
,, *Fem.* ...	〔cuneiform〕 〔cuneiform〕 〔cuneiform〕	sina ... ... 〕 sin ... 〕 sināti ... ... 〕	= *they, them*

Yā-ti (*yā-ti-ma*) and *cātu* (*că-ta*) are more substantival in their use than the other forms of the first two personal pronouns, and are generally met with as the first words of a sentence. Besides *yă-ti* we also find ⊨⊵𒌋 ⟨𒁹 *yā-si* and 𒌋 𒌋 ⟨𒁹 *ai-si*.

The Possessive Pronouns are suffixed to the Nouns and Verbs. The following is a list of them :—

POSSESSIVE PRONOUN AFFIXES OF THE NOUN.

1.	Sing. Com. Gend.	⊨⊨𒌋, 𒌋	ya, ā ... ... = *my; also* i, *as* 𒌋 ⊏ *to be read* 'āb-i, *my father*
	Plural ,,	{ 𒅋 / 𒌋 }	ni ... ...} nu ...} = *our*
2.	Sing. Masc. ...	⊱𒇻	ca, *also* -c ... = *thy*
	,, Fem.	⟨𒈨	ci ... ... = *thy*
	Plural, Masc.	𒈨 𒌋	cunu, *also* cun = *your*
	,, Fem.	[⟨𒈨 ⊱𒅀]	[cina] ... ... = *your*
3.	Sing. Masc. ...	𒈨	su, *also* -s ... = *his, its*
	,, Fem. ...	{ 𒉿 / ⟨𒁹 }	sa ... ...} si ... ...} = *her, its*
	Plural, Masc. ...	𒈨 𒌋	sunu, *also* sun = *their*
	,, Fem.	⟨𒁹 ⊱𒅀	sina, *also* sin... = *their*

Ya and *ā* were used as the pronoun suffix of the first person if the noun terminated in a vowel, *i* if it terminated in a consonant.

When the noun ends in *d, dh, t, s, ś, z,* or *ts,* the third person suffix becomes *śu, śa,* &c., as *khi-ri-it-śu* "its ditch," *bit-śu* "his house." The last letter of the noun is very frequently assimilated to the *ś* of the suffix, as *khi-ri-iś-śu, biś-su ;* and then the reduplication may be dropped, so that we get *khi-ri-śu, bi-śu.*

In the later period of the language, the possessive pronouns are attached to the substantive *at-tu* "being" or "essence," and the compound is then used as an emphatic repetition of the pronoun; thus ⟪cuneiform⟫ *zir-ya at-tū-a* = " my own race " (literally " my race (which is) mine "), ⟪cuneiform⟫ *at-tu-u-à, a-bu-u-a* " to me (was) my father."

When the accent fell on the last vowel of the noun to which the possessive pronoun was suffixed, the initial consonant of the second and third pronoun suffixes were often doubled, as ⟪cuneiform⟫ *cir-bu-us-su* " its interior," for *cirbú-su*.

POSSESSIVE PRONOUN SUFFIXES OF THE VERB.

1.	*Sing.*		-anni, -inni, -nni, -ni ...	... *Plural*	-annini, -annu, -nini, -nu
2.	,,	*Masc.*	-acca, -icca, -cca, -ca, -c	,,	-accunu, -accun, -cunu, -cun
2.	,,	*Fem.*	-acci, -icci, -cci, -ci	:,	-accina, -accin, -cina, -cin
3.	,,	*Masc.*	-assu, -issu, -su, -s	,,	-assunuti, -assunu, -assun, -sunutu (v), -sunuti (v), -sunuta (v), -sunu, -sun
3.	,,	*Fem.*	-assi, -assa, -ssa, -ssi, -sa, -si ...		-assinati, -assina, -assin, -sinatu (v), sinati (v), -sinata (v), -sina, -sin

A final *n* might be assimilated to the *initial s* of the 3rd person suffix ; thus ⟪cuneiform⟫ *in-da-na-as-su-nu-ti* " he gave them," for *inda-nan-sunuti*.

Besides *-cunu*, we also find ⟪cuneiform⟫ *cu-nu-ti*, and besides ⟪cuneiform⟫ *sunuti* and ⟪cuneiform⟫ *sinati*, we find *su-nu-siv* or *su-nu-si* and *si-na-si-iv*, just as *yāsi* appears by the side of *yāti*.

THE DEMONSTRATIVE PRONOUNS.

Sing.		Plural.

Masc.	... 𒂊𒉿𒌍	su'atu, su'ati, su'ata =*this, that* ... 𒐊𒉿𒌍 𒄿 su'atunu, su'atun, sâtunu
Fem.	... 𒀴𒉿𒌍	si'atu, ...
„	... 𒅤𒉿𒌍	sa'atu (*or* sâtu), ...⎫ 𒐊𒉿𒈨 𒁁 su'atina, satina, sa'ati, sa'ata ...⎭ sinatina
Masc.	... 𒅤𒉿𒐊	sa'asu, *or* sâsu = *this, that*... 𒅤𒐊𒄿 sâsunu, sâsun
Fem.	... 𒅤𒉿𒅤	sa'asa *or* sâsa, sa'asi ... *or* sâsi ... 𒅤𒉿𒅤𒈨 sa'asina *or* sâsina

Three demonstratives are used to determinate distance, 𒄭𒀀 *ammu* or 𒂊 *ma* ("hic") "this by me;" 𒀀𒄿 *annu* ("iste") "that by you;" and 𒂊𒆥 *'ullu* ("ille") "that by him." Of *ammu* we find only the sing. fem. 𒄭𒂊𒉿𒀀 *ammâte*, and *mâ* (𒂊𒉿) or *ma* the contracted form of the sing. masc. *amma*, and the pl. masc. *ammûta*, which is used as a suffix. Thus we have *sar Assur-ma*, "king of this same Assyria;" *anni-ma* or *an-ma*, "myself" (literally, "this person here"); 𒀀𒄿𒉿𒈨 *ina sanati-ma si'ati* "in this very year." This suffix is especially common at the end of the astrological tablets.

Sing. Masc.... an-nu	Plural, Masc.... an-nu-tu, an-nu-tav, an-ni-e
„ „ ... an-ni-i, an-ni, a-an-ni ...	„ „ ... an-nu-ti
„ „ ... an-na-a, an-na ...	
„ Fem. ... an-nă-tu, a-a-na-ti	„ Fem. ... an-na-a-ti, an-nā-tav, an-ni-ti
„ „ ... [an-ni-tu]	„ „ ... an-ne-tav, an-ni-tav, an-ni-ti
„ Masc.... ul-lu ...	„ Masc.... ul-lu-tu
„ „ ... ul-li, ul-li-e	
„ „ ... ul-la ...	
„ Fem. ... ul-lă-tu ...	„ Fem. ... [ul-la-a-tu]

From *ullu* was formed in later times the adj. 〈𒈨 𒂊 𒉌 𒉌 *ulluai* "on the further side."

In the Persian period we find a new demonstrative *'aga,* or *haga,* or *hagat*:

Sing. Masc. ... 𒉌 𒂊𒐈𒈨 'aga, 'a-ga-a, a-ga-h   *Com. gen.* ... 𒉌 𒂊𒐈𒈨 𒉌 'a-ga-a

    Fem. ... 𒉌 𒂊𒐈𒈨 𒂊𒐈 'a-gă-ta

This pronoun was further compounded with *annu* and the personal pronouns, so as to strengthen the determinative idea; thus:

Singular, Masc. ... 𒉌 𒂊𒐈𒈨 𒈨 𒐊 'agannu, 'aganna

    „   „ ... 𒉌 𒂊𒐈𒈨 𒐊 𒂊𒐈𒈨 'aga-su'u, *he namely*

Plural, Masc. ... 𒉌 𒂊𒐈𒈨 𒈨 𒐊 𒂍𒐈 'agannutu, aganutu

    „   *Fem.* ... 𒉌 𒂊𒐈𒈨 𒈨 𒐈 𒂍𒐈 'agannitu, 'aganet

    „   „ ... 𒉌 𒂊𒐈𒈨 𒐊 𒐊 'aga-sunu, *they namely*

Instead of *'aga-sū, sū-aga* also occurs, and *aga* is frequently used like a mere article.

RELATIVE PRONOUNS.

The Relative Pronoun is 𒊮 *sa*, of all numbers and genders, which was originally a demonstrative. It may be understood, as in English, "the man I saw" for "the man *whom* I saw." It is often used to express the periphrastic genitive, when instead of the construct state, the full form of the first noun with the case-ending is given followed by *sa*, which then means exactly our "of." Thus ⟨⟨ 𒔑 𒊮 𒀀 𒀀 *sarru sa matâti* "king of the world." Sometimes the first noun was omitted, as *ina sa Garganis* "according to (the maneh) of Carchemish."

The Interrogative Pronoun is ⟨⟨ ⟶ *man-nu*, 𒂊 ⟶ *mā-nu*, or ⟨⟨ *man*, "who?" "what," "which." Sometimes it is contracted into *ma-a*. *Mi-e* or *mi* also signified "who," and may be suffixed to *mannu*, forming ⟨⟨ ⟶ 𒈨 *mannu-me*, "who."

The Indefinite Pronouns are the indeclinable 𒂊 ⟶𒀜 𒂊 *ma-nam-ma*, *ma na-ma*, *man-ma*, *ma-am-man*, *ma-am-ma*, or *ma-num-ma*, "anybody," and ⟨𒀭 𒂊 *mi-im-ma*, "anything." The negative ⟶𒂊 *la* or ⟨𒂊𒀜 *ul*, joined in the same sentence with these pronouns, gave them a negative meaning, "nobody," "nothing." This negative meaning might be retained even when the accompanying negative was dropped, like *personne*, &c., in French. 𒅀 𒅀 𒂍𒐊 𒂊 *ai-um-ma* or *ya-um-ma*, with the negative understood, and 𒀭𒂊 *nin* also, signified "nobody." 𒂊 ⟶⟨ 𒂊 *matina* was "at any time," or "in any place." The indeclinable 𒂊 ⟶𒂊 *mala* = "as many as." "Some, others," was expressed by 𒅀 ⟶ 𒀲 *ā-nu-te—ā-nu-te*, and 𒅀 𒅀 ⟨𒐊𒂊 *a-kha-di—a-kha-di*. *A-kha-ri-tu* = "other," *sa-num-ma* = "another," *estin ana estin* = "one to another."

The Reflexive Pronoun is 𒂍𒅀 𒂊 ⟶ *ra-ma-nu*, *ra-ma-ni*, *ra-ma-na* "self," to which the possessive pronouns were suffixed, as *ra-ma-ni-ya* "myself," *ra-ma-nu-ca* or *ra-ma-nu-uc-ca* "thyself," *ra-ma-ni-su-un* "themselves." 𒂍𒐊𒀜 𒐊 *gadu* also was used for "individual," and "myself" might be expressed by ⟶𒀭 𒅗 𒂊 *an-ni-ma* or ⟶𒀭 𒂊 *an-ma* (literally "this (man) here").

THE VERB.

Assyrian Verbs are for the most part triliteral, that is to say, the root consists of three consonants or semi-consonants.

If the root consist of three consonants the verb is called *complete;* if one or more of the three radical letters are semi-consonants which easily pass into vowels (*h* or ℵ becoming *a; v* or ᴉ becoming *u; y* or ᴉ becoming *i;* and *e* or 𝔂 losing its guttural sound), the verb is called *defective.*

There are four principal Conjugations :—

(1) Kal, the simplest form, with an active (more rarely a neuter) signi-fication, as ⸱⸱⸱⸱ *ictum* "he concealed."

(2) Niphal, the passive of Kal, formed by prefixing *n*, which may be assimilated to the following vowel, as ⸱⸱⸱⸱ *iccatum* "he was concealed" (for *incatum*).

(3) Pael, with an intensive (and hence, sometimes a causative) significa-tion, formed by doubling the second radical letter of the root, and conjugating the persons with an inserted *u*, as ⸱⸱⸱⸱ *yucattum* (=*i-u-cattum*) "he did conceal."

(4) Shaphel, with a causative signification, formed by prefixing *s(a)* to the root, and conjugating the persons with inserted *u*, as ⸱⸱⸱⸱ *yusactum* "he caused to conceal."

Instead of Shaphel, concave verbs [*see below*] have *Aphel, s* having been changed into *h* and lost, as ⸱⸱⸱⸱ *yudhib* "he caused to be good."

Each of the four principal conjugations has two secondary forms made by inserting *t* and *tan* after the first consonant ; thus :—

(1*a*) Iphteal from Kal, as ⸱⸱⸱⸱ *ic-ta-tum.*

(1*b*) Iphtaneal from Kal, as ⸱⸱⸱⸱ *ic-tan-tum.*

(2*a*)   Ittaphal from Niphal, as ⟨cuneiform⟩ *it-ta-ctum* (for *in-ta-ctum*).

(2*b*)   Ittanaphal from Niphal, as ⟨cuneiform⟩ *it-tan-accatum* (for *in-tan-accatum*).

(3*a*)   Iphtaal from Pael, as ⟨cuneiform⟩ *yuc-ta-ltum*.

(3*b*)   Iphtanaal from Pael, as ⟨cuneiform⟩ *yuc-tan-altum*.

(4*a*)   Istaphal from Shaphel, as ⟨cuneiform⟩ *yus-ta-ctum* or *yul-ta-ctum*.

(4*b*)   Istanaphal from Shaphel, as ⟨cuneiform⟩ *yus-tan-actum* or *yul-tan-actum*.

From the Aphel of concave verbs is formed an Itaphal, as ⟨cuneiform⟩ *yu-ta-dhib*.

These secondary conjugations have a reflexive force.

Niphal and Shaphel (and also probably Aphel) admit also of *Paelised* conjugations, (2*c*) Niphael, as ⟨cuneiform⟩ *iccattum*, and (4*c*) Shaphael, as ⟨cuneiform⟩ *yuscaltum*.

From Niphal, Pael, and Shaphel, other intensive conjugations could be formed by repeating the last radical : thus (2*nd*) Niphalel, as ⟨cuneiform⟩ *iccatumĭm* ; (3*rd*) Palel, as *yucatumĭm* ; and (4*th*) Shaphalel, as *yusactumĭm*.

Except Kal and Niphal, which stood in the relation of active and passive to one another, the other conjugations had passives formed by changing the vowels of the root into *u*, thus :

(3)   Pael makes ⟨cuneiform⟩ *yucuttum* (permansive, *cuttum*).

(4)   Shaphel makes ⟨cuneiform⟩ *yus-cu-tum* (permansive, *sucutum* or *sucatum*).

     Aphel makes ⟨cuneiform⟩ *yudhub*.

(4*a*)   Istaphal makes (permansive) ⟨cuneiform⟩ *sutactim*.

The Moods are five in number—(1) the indicative, (2) the subjunctive, (3) the imperative, (4) the precative, and (5) the infinitive.

The indicative possesses two primary and three secondary TENSES—(1) the permansive or perfect; (2) the aorist or imperfect; (3) the present, a modified form of the aorist; (4) the perfect or pluperfect, the older form of the aorist; and (5) the future, the older form of the present.

The original tenses of the verb were (1) the perfect (permansive) and (2) the imperfect (aorist); but under the influence of Accadian, the imperfect split itself into two forms, one shorter (as ⟨cuneiform⟩ *iscun* "he made") and one longer (as ⟨cuneiform⟩ *isaccin* "he makes"), which came to be used with a real tense-distinction of meaning (as in Ethiopic). The longer and more primitive form of the present (*isaccinu*) came further to be used with a future force; and the longer and more primitive form of the aorist (*iscunu*), from its being adopted after words like "when" or "who," came to have generally a perfect or pluperfect sense.

The permansive (perfect) has grown out of the close attachment of abbreviated forms of the personal pronouns to nouns and participles into a true tense.

Besides the apocopated or ordinary aorist (*iscun*) and the pluperfect aorist (*iscunu*), there exists (1) a conditional or motive aorist (*iscuna*) formed by the attachment of *a*, "the augment of motion," to the apocopated aorist, and (2) the energic aorist formed by the retention of the original mimmation, *iscunum(ma)*, *iscunim(ma)*, *iscunam(ma)*. There was also another form of the aorist which ended in -*i* (as *iscuni*).

These terminations of the aorist in -*u*, -*i*, -*a*, answer to the three case-endings of the noun, the apocopated aorist corresponding with the construct state, and go back to a time when but little distinction was made between the noun and the verb. The subjunctive mood is used in relative and conditional clauses, and is denoted by the addition of the particle *ni*, which may be placed after the possessive pronoun suffix, as ⟨cuneiform⟩ *ci ikabu-su-ni* "when he had called it."

The imperative is confined to the 2nd person, the 2nd pers. sing. masc. giving the simplest form of the verb (as *sucun, rikhits, tsabat*), the vowels always being the same in both syllables, the 2nd pers. fem. ending in *i* (as *sucini* or *sucni*), the 2nd pers. pl. masc. in -*u* (as *sucinu* or *sucnu*) and the 2nd pers. pl. fem. in *ā* (as *sucinā* or *sucnā*). The 2nd pers. sing. masc. may take the augment of motion -*ă* (as *sucună* or *sucnă*). The precative is formed by prefixing *lu* or *li* (the vowel of which coalesces with the vowel of the person-prefix in the 1st and 3rd persons) to any one of the forms of the aorist. It is generally used in the 3rd person, as *liscun* "may he place." The infinitive is really a verbal substantive and declined accordingly.

Besides the moods, every conjugation possesses a participle, which, except in Kal and the Pael of concave verbs, prefixes *mu-*.

There are three *numbers*, singular, plural, and dual, but the dual which ends in -*ā* is only found in the 3rd person.

There are three Persons in the singular and plural, the 2nd and 3rd having different forms for masculine and feminine.

A feminine nominative, however, is often used improperly with a masculine verb (as 𒀭𒅖𒋻 *Istar yusapri* "the goddess Istar disclosed ") and on the other hand, in the 2nd pers. plural (especially in the imperative) we frequently find the feminine instead of the masculine form.

There are many contracted forms in the Assyrian verb, produced chiefly by dropping a short -*ĭ* or -*ă*; thus 𒁲 *tastalmi* for *tastalami*, 𒁳 *taptikdi* for *taptikidi*, *ittalcu* for *ittallicu*, *tasalmu* for *tasallimu*, *usziz* or *ulziz* for *usaziz*.

D, *ts*, *z*, or *s* assimilate the inserted *t* of the secondary conjugations, as 𒀼 *its-tsa-bat* for 𒀼 *its-ta-bat*, 𒀼 *iz-za-car* for *iz-ta-car*.

S may change the *t* into *ś* becoming *ś* itself, as 𒀼 *iś-śa-can* and *i-śa-can* for 𒀼 *is-ta-can*.

The enclitic conjunction *vă* ("and ") is attached very closely to the termination of the verb.

PARADIGMS.

The Strong or Complete Verb.

KAL.

The second vowel of the aorist may be either *a*, *i*, or *u*, as *iscun* " he placed," *ipdhir* " he freed," *itsbat* " he took," but *u* is most common.

The third vowel of the present may similarly be either *a*, *i*, or *u*, as *inaccar* " he estranges," *isaccin* "he places," *idammum* " it passes away," but *i* is, by far, the most common vowel.

The first person singular of the aorist sometimes has *e* in Babylonian instead of *a*, as 〈〈〈 ⟨⊢⟩⟨⊣⟩ *esnik* for *asnik*, and verbs א"פ (see *infra*) in Assyrian might adopt the same vowel.

PERMANSIVE [*or* Perfect].—*Singular.*			PRESENT.—*Singular.*		
I.	⊢⟨⊨ ⊢⟨ 🔲	sac-na-cu *or* sac-na-ac	𝌆 ⊢⟨⊨ ⊲⊨	a-sac-cin "*I place*"	
2. *Masc.*	,,	,, sac-na at	,,	,, ta-sac-sin	
2. *Fem.*	,,	,, [? sac-na-ti]	,,	,, ta-sac-ci-ni	
3. *Masc.*	,,	,, sa-cin (Ⴤ ⊲⊨)	,,	,, i-sac-cin	
3. *Fem.*	,,	,, sac-nat	,,	,, ta-sac-cin	

			Plural.		
				Plural.	
I.	,,	,, ?	⊨⊣⟨⊨ ⊲⊨	ni-sac-cin	
2. *Masc.*	,,	,, ?	,,	,, ta-sac-ci-nu	
2. *Fem.*	,,	,, ?	,,	,, ta-sac-ci-na	
3. *Masc.*	,,	,, sac-nu	,,	,, i-sac-ci-nu	
3. *Fem.*	,,	,, sac-na	,,	,, i-sac-ci-na	

			Dual.		*Dual.*
3.	⊢⟨⊨ ⊢⟨ 𝌆	sac-na-a [sacnā] ...	,,	,,	[i-sac-ci-na-a]

AORIST.

Singular.

1.	𒀀	as-cun		ar-khi-its			ats-bat	
		("*I placed*") ;		("*I inundated*") ;			("*I took*")	
2. *Masc.*	,,	,,	tas-cun ;	,,	,,	tar-khi-its ;	,,	,,	ta-ats-bat
2. *Fem.*	,,	,,	tas-cu-ni ;	,,	,,	tar-khi-tsi ;	,,	,,	ta-ats-ba-ti
3. *Masc.*	,,	,,	is-cun ;	,,	,,	ir-khi-its ;	,,	..	its-bat
3. *Fem.*	,,	,,	tas-cun ;	,,	,,	tar-khi-its ;	,,	,,	ta-ats-bat

Plural.

1.		ni-is-cun ;		ni-ir-khi-its ;			ni-its-bat	
2. *Masc.*	,,	,,	tas-cu-nu ;	,,	,,	tar-khi-tsu ;	,,	,,	ta-ats-ba-tu
2. *Fem.*	,,	,,	tas-cu-na ;	,,	,,	tar-khi-tsa ;	,,	,,	ta-ats-ba-ta
3. *Masc.*	,,	,,	is-cu-nu ;	,,	,,	ir-khi-tsu ;	,,	,,	its-ba-tu
3. *Fem.*	,,	,,	is-cu-na ;	,,	,,	ir-khi-tsa ;	,,	,,	its-ba-ta

Dual.

3.	{ is-cu-na-a / [iscunâ]; }	ir-khi-tsa-a ;	its-ba-ta-a

The student will form the future and pluperfect by attaching the vowel -*u* to those singular forms of the present and aorist which end in a consonant, and -*uni* (also -*unu*, -*unuv*, and -*univ*) to those plural forms of the same tenses which end in a consonant.

IMPERATIVE.

Sing. 2. *Masc.*		su-cun ;		ri-khi-its ;		tsa-bat	
,, 2. *Fem.*	,,	,,	su-ci-ni *or* su-uc-ni ;	,,	,,	ri-khi-tsi *or* ri-ikh-tsi ;	,,	tsa-ba-ti *or* tsa-ab-ti
Plu. 2. *Masc.*	,,	,,	su-ci-nu *or* su-uc-nu ;	,,	,,	ri-khi-tsu *or* ri-ikh-tsu ;	,,	tsa-ba-tu *or* tsa-ab-tu
,, 2. *Fem.*	,,	,,	su-ci-na *or* su-uc-na ;	,,	,,	ri-khi-tsa *or* ri-ikh-tsa ;	,,	tsa-ba-ta *or* tsa-ab-ta

PRECATIVE.

Singular.

1. 𒀭 lu-us-cun; 𒀭 lu-ur-khi-its; 𒀭 lu-uts-bat
2. *Masc.* „ „ lu-tas-cun; „ „ lu-tar-khi-its; „ „ lu-ta-ats-bat
3. *M. & F.* „ „ li-is-cun; „ „ li-ir-khi-its; „ „ li-its-bat

Plural.

3. *Masc.* 𒀭 li-is-cu-nu; 𒀭 li-ir-khi-tsu;
3. *Fem.* „ „ li-is-cu-na; „ „ li-ir-khi-tsa;
3. *Masc.* 𒀭 li-its-ba-tu
3. *Fem.* „ „ li-its-ba-ta

The augment of motion and the mimmation may be attached to all the above forms. When the augment of motion is attached to the 2nd person masc. plur. of the imperative *u*+*a* passes through *va* into *ā*; thus 𒀭 *su-uc-nā* (or 𒀭 *su-uc-na-a*) instead of *su-uc-nu-a*.

INFINITIVE.

𒀭 sā-cā-nu *to dwell.*
𒀭 ra-kha-tsu *to inundate.*
𒀭 tsa-ba-tu *to seize.*

PARTICIPLE.

𒀭 sā-ci-nu *dwelling.*
𒀭 rā-khi-tsu *inundating.*
𒀭 tsā-bi-tu *seizing.*

IPHTEAL.

PERMANSIVE (Perfect).				PRESENT.		
Singular.				*Singular.*		
I.	𒀹𒌋𒀭𒁹 𒁹	sit-cu-na-cu ...		𒈨𒈨𒈨		as-tac-can
				𒈨𒈨𒈨		as-ta-can
				𒈨𒈨𒈨		al-ta-can
2. *Masc.*	„ „	[sit-cu-na-at] ...		„	„	tas-tac-can, *&c.*
2. *Fem.*	„ „	?		„	„	tas-tac-ca-ni
3. *Masc.*	„ „	sit-cun ...		„	„	is-tac-can
3. *Fem.*	„ „	sit-cu-nat ...		„	„	tas-tac-can
Plural.				*Plural.*		
I.	„ „	?		𒀹 𒈨 𒈨		nis-tac-can
2. *Masc.*	„ „	? ...		„	„	tas-tac-ca-nu
2. *Fem.*	„ „	? ...		„	„	tas-tac-ca-na
3. *Masc.*	„ „	sit-cu-nu ...		„	„	is-tac-ca-nu
3. *Fem.*	„ „	sit-cu-na ...		„	„	is-tac-ca-na
Dual.				*Dual.*		
3.	„ „	[sit-cu-na-a] ...				[is-tac-ca-na-a]

AORIST.

				Singular.			
I.	𒈨 𒈨 𒈨	as-ta-cin, al-ta-cin ;		𒈨 𒈨 𒈨		ap-te-kid "*I overlooked*"
2. *Masc.*	„ „	tas-ta-cin, *&c.;*		„	„	ta-ap-te-kid
3. *Fem.*	„ „	tas-ta-ci-ni ;		„	„	ta-ap-te-ki-di
3. *Masc.*	„ „	is-ta-cin ;		„	„	ip-te-kid
3. *Fem.*	„ „	tas-ta-cin ;		„	„	ta-ap-te-kid

				Plural.			
I.	𒀹 𒈨 𒈨	nis-ta-cin ;		𒈨 𒈨 𒈨 𒈨		ni-ip-te-kid
2. *Masc.*	„ „	tas-ta-ci-nu ;		„	„	ta-ap-te-ki-du
2. *Fem.*	„ „	tas-ta-ci-na ;		„	„	tap-te-ki-da
3. *Masc.*	„ „	is-ta-ci-nu ;		„	„	ip-te-ki-du
3. *Fem.*	„ „	is-ta-ci-na ;		„	„	ip-te-ki-da

				Dual.			
3.	„ „	[is-ta-ci-na-a]		„	„	[ip-te-ki-da-a]

IPHTEAL—*continued.*

IMPERATIVE.

	Singular.			*Plural.*	
2. *Masc.*	𒐏𒐏	sit-cin		𒐏𒐏	sit-ci-nu
2. *Fem.*	„ „	sit-ci-ni		„ „	sit-ci-na

PRECATIVE.
Singular.

1.	𒐏𒐏𒐏	lu-us-ta-can ;	𒐏𒐏𒐏	lu-up-te-kdi
3.	„ „	li-is-ta-can ;	„ „	li-ip-te-kid

Plural.

3. *M.*	𒐏𒐏𒐏	li-is-ta-ca-nu ;	𒐏𒐏𒐏	li-ip-te-ki-du
3. *F.*	„ „	li-is-ta-ca-na ;	„ „	li-ip-te-ki-da

INFINITIVE.

𒐏𒐏 sit-cu-nu ; 𒐏𒐏 pit-ku-du

PARTICIPLE.

𒐏𒐏 mus-ta-ca-nu, mul-ta-ca-nu
𒐏𒐏 mu-up-te-ki-du

NIPHAL.

PERMANSIVE (Perfect).			PRESENT.		
Singular.			*Singular.*		
1.	...	[na-as-cu-na-cu]	𒀸 𒀹 𒀸		as-sa-can
2. *Masc.*	...	[na-as-cu-na-at]	,, ,,		tas-sa-can
2. *Fem.*	... ...	?	,, ,,		tas-sa-ca-ni
3. *Masc.*	𒀭𒀸✛𒀀𒈨	na-as-cun	,, ,,		is-sa-ca-an
3. *Fem.*	,, ,,	[na-as-cu-nat]	,, ,,		tas-sa-can
Plural.			*Plural.*		
1.	? ,, ,,		𒀹 𒀭𒀹 𒀹 𒀸		ni-is-sa-can
2. *Masc.*	? ,, ,, ...		,, ,,		tas-sa-ca-nu
2. *Fem.*	? ,, ,, ...		,, ,,		tas-sa-ca-na
3. *Masc.*	𒀭𒀸𒂖✛	na-as-cu-nu	𒀭𒀹 𒀹 𒀭𒂖✛		is-sa-ca-nu
3. *Fem.*	,, ,,	na-as-cu-na	,, ,,		is-sa-ca-na
Dual.			*Dual.*		
3.		[na-as-cu-na-a]	,, ,,		[is-sa-ca-na-a]

IMPERATIVE.			PRECATIVE.		
Singular.			*Singular.*		
2. *Masc.*	𒀭𒀸𒀸𒀸	na-as-cin	1.	𒂖𒀹𒀹𒀹𒀸	lu-us-sa-cin
2. *Fem.*	,, ,,	na-as-ci-ni	3.	,, ,,	li-is-sa-cin
Plural.			*Plural.*		
2. *Masc.*	,,	na-as-ci-nu	3. *Masc.*	,, ,,	lis-sa-ci-nu, lis-sac-nu
2. *Fem.*	,, ,,	na-as-ci-na	3. *Fem.*	,, ,,	lis-sa-ci-na, lis-sac-na

AORIST.		
Singular.		
1.	𒀸 𒀹 𒀸𒀸	as-sa-cin, as-sa-cun
2. *Masc.*	,, ,,	tas-sa-cin, tas-sa-cun
2. *Fem.*	,, ,,	tas-sa-ci-ni, tas-sa-cu-ni
3. *Masc.*	,, ,,	is-sa-cin, is-sa-cun
3. *Fem.*	,, ,,	tas-sa-cin, tas-sa-cun

AORIST—*Continued.*

Plural.

1.			na-as-sa-cin, na-as-sa-cun
2. *Masc.*	,,	,,	tas-sa-ci-nu, tas-sa-cu-nu
2. *Fem.*	,,	,,	tas-sa-ci-na, tas-sa-cu-na
3. *Masc.*	,.	,;	is-sa-ci-nu, is-sa-cu-nu
3. *Fem.*	,,	,,	is-sa-ci-na, is-sa-cu-na

Dual.

3.	,,	,,	[is-sa-ci-na-a]

INFINITIVE.

na-as-ca-a-nu [nascānu]

PARTICIPLE.

mu-se-es-sa-ci-nu [musessacinu]

ISTAPHAL.

PERMANSIVE (*or* Perfect).		PRESENT.	
Singular.		*Singular.*	
I. [na-as-te-cu-na-cu?], &c.		I. at-ta-as-can, &c.	

IMPERATIVE.		PRECATIVE.	
Singular.		*Singular.*	
2. *Masc.* ni-tas-cin (?), &c. ...		3. „ „ li-it-tas-cin, &c.	

AORIST.	INFINITIVE.	PARTICIPLE.
Singular.	na-at-sa-cā-nu	mut-tas-ca-nu
I. at-ta-as-cin at-ta-as-cun, &c.		

PAEL.

	PERMANSIVE (*or* Perfect).				PRESENT	
	Singular.				*Singular.*	
I.	sac-ca-na-cu			I.	u-sac-can	
2. *Masc.*	„ „ [sac-ca-na-at]			2. *Masc.*	„ „ tu-sac-can	
2. *Fem.*	„ „ ?			2. *Fem.*	„ „ tu-sac-ca-ni, tu-sac-ni	
3. *Masc.*	sac-can			3. *Masc.*	„ „ yu-sac-can	
3. *Fem.*	„ sac-ca-nat			3. *Fem.*	„ „ tu-sac-can	
	Plural.				*Plural.*	
I.	... ?			I.	nu-sac-can	
2. *Masc.*	... ?			2. *Masc.*	„ „ tu-sac-ca-nu	
2. *Fem.*	... ?			2. *Fem.*	„ „ tu-sac-ca-na	
3. *Masc.*	... sac-ca-nu			3. *Masc.*	„ „ yu-sac-ca-nu	
3. *Fem*	... [sac-ca-na]			3. *Fem.*	„ „ yu-sac-ca-na	
	Dual.				*Dual.*	
3.	... [sac-ca-na-a]			3.	„ „ [yu-sac-ca-na-a]	

	IMPERATIVE.	PRECATIVE.
	Singular.	*Singular.*
2. *Masc.*	𒀭 suc-cin (su-cin)	1. lu-sac-can
2. *Fem.*	,, suc-ci-ni	3. ,, ,, lu-sac-can, lu-sac-cin
	Plural.	*Plural.*
2. *Masc.*	suc-ci-nu	3. *Masc.* lu-sac-ca-nu
2. *Fem.*	,, suc-ci-na	3. *Fem.* ,, ,, lu-sac-ca-na

AORIST.

	Singular.			*Plural.*	
1.		u-sac-cin	1.		nu-sac-cin
		u-sac-cun	2. *Masc.*	,, ,,	tu-sac-ci-nu
		u-sic-cin	2. *Fem.*	,, ,,	tu-sac-ci-na
2. *Masc.*	,, ,,	tu-sac-cin	3. *Masc.*	,, ,,	yu-sac-ci-nu
		tu-sac-cun	3. *Fem.*	,, ,,	yu-sac-ci-na
		tu-sic-sin		*Dual.*	
2. *Fem.*	,, ,,	tu-sac-si-ni, &c.	3.	,, ,,	[yu-sac-ci-na-a]
3. *Masc.*	,, ,,	yu-sac-cin			
3. *Fem.*	,, ,,	tu-sac-cin			

INFINITIVE.	PARTICIPLE.
sac-cā-nu [*but the infin. passive is more common*]	mu-sac-ci-nu
Infin. pass. suc-cu-nu	

From its intensive signification Pael comes sometimes to be used in a causative sense. When Kal is intransitive, Pael is transitive.

N.B.—The present and aorist of Pael are distinguished from the present of Kal by the vowel *u* in the first syllable.

The reduplication is often neglected in writing. It is sometimes replaced in the case of labials and dentals by *mb* (*mp*) and *nd* (*ndh*, *nt*).

IPHTAEL.

PERMANSIVE. *Not found.*

PRESENT.

	Singular.				Plural.	
1.	𒀭 𒀭 𒀭	us-tac-can		𒀭 𒀭 𒀭 𒀭	nu-us-tac-can	
2. *Masc.*	,,	,,	tu-us-tac-can	,,	,,	tu-us-tac-ca-nu
2. *Fem.*	,,	,,	tu-us-tac-ca-ni	,,	,,	tu-us-tac-ca-na
3. *Masc.*	,,	,,	yus-tac-can	𒀭 𒀭 𒀭 𒀭	yus-tac-ca-nu	
3. *Fem.*	,,	,,	tu-us-tac-can	,,	,,	yus-tac-ca-na

Dual.

,,   ,,   [yus-tac-ca-na-a]

AORIST.

Singular.

1.	𒀭 𒀭 𒀭	us-tac-cin ;		𒀭 𒀭 𒀭	up-te-kid	
2. *Masc.*	,,	,,	tu-us-tac-cin ;	,,	,,	tu-up-te-kid
2. *Fem.*	,,	,,	tu-us-tac-cin ;	,,	,,	tu-up-te-ki-di
3. *Masc.*	,,	,,	yus-tac-cin ;	,,	,,	yup-te-kid
3. *Fem.*	,,	,,	tu-us-tac-cin ;	,,	,,	tu-up-te-kid

Plural.

1.	𒀭 𒀭 𒀭 𒀭	nu-us-tac-cin ;		𒀭 𒀭 𒀭 𒀭	nu-up-te-kid	
2. *Masc.*	,,	,,	tu-us-tac-ci-nu ;	,,	,,	tu-up-te-ki-du
2. *Fem.*	,,	,,	tu-us-tac-ci-na ;	,,	,,	tu-up-te-ki-da
3. *Masc.*	𒀭 𒀭 𒀭 𒀭	yus-tac-ci-nu ;		𒀭 𒀭 𒀭 𒀭	yup-te-ki-du
3. *Fem.*	,,	,,	yus-tac-ci-na ;	,,	,,	yup-te-ki-da

Dual.

3.   ,,   ,,   [yus-tac-ci-na-a]

IPHTAEL—*continued* .

IMPERATIVE. *Not found.*

PRECATIVE.

Singular.		*Plural.*
3. 𒀭𒈾𒊏𒈾 lu-us-tac-can	3. *Masc.* 𒀭𒈾𒊏𒈾𒈾 lu-us-tac-ca-nu	
	3. *Fem.* „ . „ lu-us-tac-ca-na	

INFINITIVE.	PARTICIPLE.
[sa-tac-cā-nu]	𒈬𒌋𒍑 mus-tac-ci-nu

SHAPHEL.

PERMANSIVE. *Not found.*

PRESENT.		AORIST.	
Singular.		*Singular.*	
1. 〖cuneiform〗 u-sa-as-can		1. 〖cuneiform〗 u-sa-as-cin, u-se-es-cin	
2. *Masc.* 〖cuneiform〗 tu-sa-as-can		2. *Masc.* ,, ,, tu-sa-as-cin,&c.	
2. *Fem.* ,, ,, tu-sa-as-ca-ni		2. *Fem.* ,, ,, tu-sa-as-ci-ni	
3. *Masc.* ,, ,, yu-sa-as-can		3. *Masc.* ,, ,, yu-sa-as-cin	
3. *Fem.* ,, ,, tu-sa-as-can		3. *Fem.* ,, ,, tu-sa-as-cin	
Plural.		*Plural.*	
1. 〖cuneiform〗 nu-sa-as-can		1. 〖cuneiform〗 nu-sa-as-cin	
2. *Masc.* ,, ,, tu-sa-as-ca-nu		2. *Masc.* ,, ,, tu-sa-as-ci-nu	
2. *Fem.* ,, ,, tu-sa-as-ca-na		2. *Fem.* ,, ,, tu-sa-as-ci-na	
3. *M.* 〖cuneiform〗 yu-sa-as-ca-nu		3. *Masc.* ,, ,, yu-sa-as-ci-nu	
3. *Fem.* ,, ,, yu-sa-as-ca-na		3. *Fem.* ,, ,, yu-sa-as-ci-na	
Dual.		*Dual.*	
3. [yu-sa-as-ca-na-a]		3. [yu-sa-as-ci-na-a]	

IMPERATIVE.		PRECATIVE.	
Singular.		*Singular.*	
2. *Masc.* 〖cuneiform〗 su-us-cin		1. lu-sa-as-cin	
2. *Fem.* ,, ,, su-us-ci-ni		3. lu-sa-as-can	
Plural.		*Plural.*	
2. *Masc.* ,, ,, su-us-ci-nu		3. *M.* 〖cuneiform〗 lu-sa-as-ci-nu	
2. *Fem.* ,, ,, su-us-ci-na		3. *Fem.* ,, ,, lu-sa-as-ci-na	

INFINITIVE.

〖cuneiform〗 sa-as-cā-nu [*but the Infin. passive is more common*]. 〖cuneiform〗 su-us-cu-nu

PARTICIPLE.

〖cuneiform〗 mu-sa-as-ci-nu

ISTAPHAL.

PERMANSIVE. *Not found.*

PRESENT. Singular.		AORIST. Singular.	
1. 𒀭𒌓𒐊 us-tas-can *or* ul-tas-can, &c.		1. us-tas-cin *or* ul-tas-cin 𒀭𒌓𒐊, {us ul}-te-sib, &c.	

IMPERATIVE. Singular.		PRECATIVE. Singular.	
2. *Masc.* 𒀭𒌓𒐊 su-ti-is-cin, &c.		3. 𒀭𒌓𒐊 lu-us-tas-can, &c.	

INFINITIVE PASSIVE.

𒀭𒌓𒐊 su-te-es-cu-nu.

PARTICIPLE.

𒀭𒌓𒐊 mus-tas-ci-nu ; 𒀭𒌓𒐊 mul-tas-ci-nu.

THE WEAK OR DEFECTIVE VERBS.

If one of the radicals of a verb is *n*, *á*, *h*, *u* (*v*), *i* (*y*) or *e*, it differs in many particulars from the conjugation of the Strong Verb, owing to the assimilation of these letters to other vowels or consonants.

Verbs which begin with these letters are called verbs פ״נ, פ״א, פ״ה, פ״ו, פ״י, and פ״ע; verbs which end with them are called verbs ל״נ, ל״א, ל״ה, ל״ו, ל״י, and ל״ע; verbs which have one of these letters as a second radical are called verbs ע״נ, ע״א, ע״ה, ע״ו, ע״י, and ע״ע. The last class of verbs are also called Concave Verbs.

Verbs פ״נ.

N is assimilated to the following letter; though in some few instances we find it irregularly retained. Before *b* or *p* it may be changed to *m*.

	PERMANSIVE.		PRESENT.	
Kal	... 𒀭 𒈨𒌑	na-mir, "*he sees*"	𒂍 𒅆𒆠 𒈨𒌑	i-nam-mir *or* i-nam-mar
Iphteal	... 𒈾 𒄿𒌆 𒈠	ni-it-mur	„ „	it-ta-mar
Niphal	𒅗 𒈠	nam-mur	„ „	in-na-mar
Ittaphal	„ „	[na-at-te-mur]	𒄿𒌆 𒀸 𒅅	it-tam-mar
Pael	... 𒅗 𒅅	nam-mar	„ „	yu-nam-mar
Iphtaal	„ „	...	𒀸 𒀸 𒅅	yut-tam-mar
Shaphel	„ „	[sam-mar]	„ „	yu-sam-mar
Istaphal	„ „	[sat-ne-mar]	„ „	yus-tam-mar
Shaphael	„ „	[sa-nam-mar]	„ „	yus-nam-mar
Istaphael	„ „		„ „	yus-te-nam-mar
	PASSIVE.		PASSIVE.	
Pael	𒄿 𒅅	num-mur	„ „	yu-num-mar
Iphtaal	... „ „		„ „	yut-tum-mar
Shaphel	... { 𒂍 𒌋 𒅅	su-nu-mur }	„ „	yu-sa-nu-mar
	{ 𒂍 𒀭 𒅅	su-na-mur }		
Istaphal	... 𒂍 𒀸 𒌋 𒅅	su-te-nu-mur	„ „	yus-tum-mar
Shaphael	... { 𒂍 𒄿 𒅅	su-num-mur		
	{ 𒂍 𒅗 𒅅	su-nam-mur	„ „	yus-num-mar

		AORIST.			IMPERATIVE.	
Kal	...	𒀸𒌋𒌋	im-mur	"*he saw*"	𒀸𒌋	u-mur *or* a-mur
"		𒀸𒌋	id-din	"*he gave*"	𒀸𒌋	i-din.
"	...	𒀸𒌋	ip-pal	"*he threw down*"	"	a-pal.
"	...	𒀸𒌋	e-cil	"*he ate*"	"	e-cil
Iphteal		𒀸𒌋 𒀸𒌋 𒀸𒌋	it-ta-mir		"	ni-it-mir
Niphal	...	𒀸𒌋 𒀸𒌋 𒀸𒌋	in-na-mir		"	nam-mir
Ittaphal		"	"	it-tam-mir	"	[ni-tam-mir]
Pael		"	"	yu-nam-mir	"	nu-um-mir
Iphtaal		"	"	yut-tam-mir	—	
Shaphel		"	"	yu-sam-mir	"	su-um-mir
Istaphal		"	"	yus-tam-mir	"	su-ut-tim-mir
Shaphael		"	"	yus-nam-mir	"	su-num-mir
Istaphael		"	"	yus-te-nam-mir	—	

		PASSIVE.			PASSIVE.
Pael		𒀸𒌋 𒀸𒌋 𒀸𒌋	yu-num-mir		—
Iphtaal		"	"	yut-tum-mur	—
Shaphel		"	"	{yu-sa-nu-mur / yus-nu-mur}	—
Istaphal		"	"	yus-tum-mur	—
Shaphael		"	"	yus-num-mur	—

PARTICIPLE.

Kal	...	𒀸𒌋 𒀸𒌋 𒀸𒌋	nā-mi-ru, nam-ru
Iphteal	...	𒀸𒌋 𒀸𒌋 𒀸𒌋 𒀸𒌋	mut-ta-mi-ru
Niphal		𒀸𒌋 𒀸𒌋 𒀸𒌋 𒀸𒌋 𒀸𒌋	mu-un-nam-mi-ru, mun-nam-ru
Ittaphal		𒀸𒌋 𒀸𒌋 𒀸𒌋 𒀸𒌋	mut-ta-ma-ru
Pael	...	𒀸𒌋 𒀸𒌋 𒀸𒌋 𒀸𒌋	mu-nam-mi-ru
Iphtaal	...	𒀸𒌋 𒀸𒌋 𒀸𒌋 𒀸𒌋	mut-tam-mi-ru
Shaphel		𒀸𒌋 𒀸𒌋 𒀸𒌋 𒀸𒌋	mu-sam-mi-ru
Istaphal		𒀸𒌋 𒀸𒌋 𒀸𒌋 𒀸𒌋	mus-tam-mi-ru
Shaphael		𒀸𒌋 𒀸𒌋 𒀸𒌋 𒀸𒌋	mus-nam-mi-ru
Istaphael		𒀸𒌋 𒀸𒌋 𒀸𒌋 𒀸𒌋 𒀸𒌋	mus-te-nam-mi-ru

Verbs א"פ.

KAL.

PERMANSIVE.		PRESENT.		AORIST.	
Sing. 1.	[asabacu]	𒀀𒀝 a-sab "*I sit*"		𒀀 a-sib, 𒀀 c-sib	
				,, a-cul, ,, c-cul	
,, 2. *Masc.* ... [asabat]		,, ta-sab		,, ta-sib	
,, 2. *Fem.* ... —		,, ta-sa-bi		,, ta-si-bi	
,, 3. *Masc.* ... [a-sab]		,, ya-sab, i-sab		,, ya-sib, i-sib 𒀀	
,, 3. *Fem.* ... —		,, ta-sab		,, ta-sib	
Plur. ... —		𒈾 na-sab		𒈾 na-sib	
,, 2. *Masc.* ... —		,, ta-sa-bu		,, ta-si-bu	
,, 2. *Fem.* ... —		,, ta-sa-ba		,, ta-si-ba	
,, 3. *Masc.* ... a-sa-bu		,, ya-sa-bu, i-sa-bu		,, ya-si-bu, i-si-bu	
,, 3. *Fem.* ... [a-sa-ba]		,, ya-sa-ba, i-sa-ba		,, ya-si-ba, i-si-ba	
Dual, 3. ... [asabā]		,, [ya-sa-bū]		,, ya-si-bā]	

IMPERATIVE AND PRECATIVE.

Sing. 1.	𒂊 li-su-ub,	𒇷 lu-sib
,, 2. *Masc.* ... ,, ,,	c-sib, a-cul	
,, 2. *Fem.* ... ,, ,,	e-si-bi, a-cu-li	
,, 3. *Masc.* ... ,, ,,	li-su-ub, lu-sib	
,, 3. *Fem.* ,, ,,	---	
Plur. 1. ... ,, ,,	—	
,, 2. *Masc.* ... 𒂊 c-si-bu,	𒀀 a-cu-la	
,, 2. *Fem.* ,, ,,	e-si-bu, a-cu-la	
,, 3. *Masc.* ... ,, ,,	li-su-bu, lu-si-bu	
,, 3 *Fem.* ... ,, ,,	li-su-ba, lu-si-ba	

INFINITIVE.		PARTICIPLE.	
𒀀	sa-a-bu	𒀀 ...	a-si-bu

PARADIGM OF THE OTHER CONJUGATIONS.

	PERMANSIVE.				PRESENT.		
Iphteal	𒀹 𒂍 𒐊		te-sub	𒌋 𒐊𒌋𒌋 𒌋𒑲			i-ta-sab
Niphal	„	„	[nā-sub]		„	„	i-na-sab
Ittaphal	„	„	—		„	„	it-te-sab
Pael	„	„	[assab]		„	„	yu-as-ab, yus-sab
Iphtaal	„	„	—		„	„	yu-tas-sab
Shaphel	„	„	[sāsab]		„	„	yu-sa-sab, yu-se-sab
Istaphal	„	„	[satesab]		„	„	yus-te-sab yul-te-sab
Itaphal ...	„	„	—		„	„	yu-te-sab
Pael Pass. ...	„	„	us-sub		„	„	yu-us-sab
Istaphal Pass.	„	„	su-te-sub		„	„	[yus-tu-sab]

	AORIST.			IMPERATIVE.	PARTICIPLE.		
Iphteal ...	𒌋 𒐊𒌋𒌋 𒐊		i-ta-sib	[it-sib]	𒀹 𒐊𒌋𒌋 𒌋 𒀹		mu-ta-sa-bu
Niphal ...	„	„	i-na-sib	na-sib	„	„	mu-na-si-bu
Ittaphal ...	„	„	it-te-sib	—	„	„	mut-te-si-bu
Pael ...	„	„	yu-as-sib, yus-sib	[us-sib]	„	„	mus-si-bu
Iphtaal ...	„	„	yu-tas-sib	[i-ta-sab]	„	„	mut-tas-sa-bu
Shaphel ...	„	„	yu-sa-sib, yu-se-sib	su-sib	„	„	mu-se-si-bu
Istaphal ...	„	„	yus-te-sib, yul-te-sib	su-te-sib	„	„	mus-te-si-bu
Itaphal ...	„	„	yu-te-sib	[u-te-sib]	„	„	mu-te-si-bu
Pael Pass.	„	„	yu-us-sub	—	—		
Istaphal Pass.	„	„	[yus-tu-sub]	—	—		

Verbs פ״ה

KAL.

PERMANSIVE.

	Singular.	
1.		[ha-la-ca-cu]
2. *Masc.*		[ha-la-ca-at]
2. *Fem.*	…	…
3. *Masc.*	ha-lac	…
3. *Fem.*	…	…

	Plural.	
1. *Masc.*	…	…
2. *Fem.*	…	…
2. *Masc.*		ha-la-cu
3. *Fem.*		[ha-la-ca]

	Dual.	
3.		ha-la-ca-a …

PRESENT.

	Singular.	
1.	al-lac	…
2. *Masc.*	a-lac "I go"	…
	a-ha-bid "I destroy"	…
2. *Fem.*	tal-lac, &c.	…
2. *Masc.*	tal-la-ci	…
3. *Masc.*	il-lac	…
3. *Fem.*	tal-lac	…

	Plural.	
1.	na-al-lac	…
2. *Masc.*	tal-la-cu	…
2. *Fem.*	tal-la-ca	…
3. *Masc.*	il-la-cu	…
3. *Fem.*	il-la-ca	…

	Dual.	
3.	[illacā]	…

AORIST.

	Singular.	
	a-lic	
	al-lic	
	ah-bid	
	tal-lic, &c.	
	tal-li-ci	
	il-lic	
	tal-lic	

	Plural.	
	na-al-lic	
	tal-li-cu	
	tal-li-ca	
	il-li-cu	
	il-li-ca	

	Dual.	
	[lilicā]	

IMPERATIVE AND PRECATIVE.

	Singular.	
1.	lil-lic	
	li-lic	
2. *Masc.*	ha-lic	
2. *Fem.*	(h)al-ci	
3. *Masc.*	lil-lic li-lic	

	Plural.	
2. *Masc.*	(h)al-cu	
2. *Fem.*	(h)al-ca	
3. *Masc.*	lil-li-cu li-li-cu	
3. *Fem.*	lil-li-cu, li-li-ca	

INFINITIVE.

la-cu

PARTICIPLE.

(h)al-li-cu

(h)a-li-cu

PARADIGM OF THE OTHER CONJUGATIONS.

PERMANSIVE.		PRESENT.		AORIST.	
Iphteal		𒀸 𒂎 𒈠 i-tal-lac		𒀸 𒂎 𒈾 i-tal-lic	
„		𒉺 𒈨 𒈠 it-ta-lac	„	„ it-ta-lic
Niphal ...	[nal-luc]	„	„ i-na-al-lac	„	„ i-na-al-lic
Ittaphal ...		„	„ it-tal-lac	„	„ it-tal-lic
Pael	al-lac	„	„ yu-'al-lac	„	„ yu-'al-lic
„	„	„	„ yul-lac	„	„ yul-lic
Iphtaal ...		„	„ yu-tal-lac	„	„ yu-tal-lic
Shaphel ...	[sal-lac]	„	„ yu-sal-lac	„	„ yu-sal-lic
Istaphel ...		„	„ yus-tal-lac	„	„ yus-tal-lic

IMPERATIVE.		PARTICIPLE.	
Iphteal	[it-lic]	𒀸 𒂎 𒈨 𒂍 mu-tal-la-cu	
Niphal	na-al-lic	„ , mu-na-al-li-cu
Ittaphal		„ „ mut-tal-li-cu
Pael ...	(h)ul-lic	„ „ mu-'al-li-cu
Iphtaal ...	[i-tal-lic]	„ „ mu-tal-li-cu
Shaphal ...	sul-lic	„ „ mu-sal-li-cu
Istaphal	[su-tal-lic]	„ „ mus-tal-li-cu

Verbs פ"ו.

KAL.

PERMANSIVE.	PRESENT.	AORIST.	IMPERATIVE AND PRECATIVE.
Singular.	Singular.	Singular.	Singular.
1. [u-la-da-cu]	u-lad	u-lid, "I begat"	lu-lid
2. Masc.	,, ,, tu-lad	,, ,, tu-lid	,, ,, lid
2. Fem.	,, ,, tu-la-di	,, ,, tu-li-di	,, ,, li-di
3. Masc. [u-lid] ...	yu-lad	yu-lid	,, ,, lu-lid
3. Fem.	,, ,, tu-lad	,, ,, tu-lid	
Plural.	**Plural.**	**Plural.**	**Plural.**
1.	,, ,, nu-lad	,, ,, nu-lid	
2. Masc.	,, ,, tu-la-du	,, ,, tu-li-du	,, ,, li-du
2. Fem.	,, ,, tu-la-da	,, ,, tu-li-da	,, ,, li-da
3. Masc. ...	,, ,, yu-la-du	,, ,, yu-li-du	,, ,, lu-li-du
3. Fem. ...	,, ,, yu-la-da	,, ,, yu-li-da	,, ,, lu-li-da
Dual	**Dual.**	**Dual.**	
3. ...	,, ,, [yu-la-da-a]	,, ,, [yulidā]	

INFINITIVE.	PARTICIPLE.
a-la-du	u-li-du
lā-du	a-li-du.

PARADIGM OF THE OTHER CONJUGATIONS.

PERMANSIVE.		PRESENT.		AORIST.	
Iphteal ...	[telud]		i-tu-lad		i-tu-lid
Niphal ...	[nulud]	,, ,,	[i-ne-lad]	,, ,,	[i-ne-lid]
Ittaphal ...		,, ,,	i-tu-lad	,, ,,	it-tu-lid
Pael	[ullad]	,, ,,	{ yu-'ul-lad / yul-lad }	,, ,,	{ yu-'ul-lid / yul-lid }
Iphtaal ...		,, ,,	yu-tul-lad	,, ,,	yu-tul-lid
Shaphel ...	[sulad]	,, ,,	yu-se-lad	,, ,,	yu-se-lid
Istaphal ...	[sutelad]	,, ,,	yus-te-lad	,, ,,	yus-te lid

IMPERATIVE.		PARTICIPLE.
Iphteal		mu-ta-li-du
Niphal	... nu-lid	mu-ne-li-du
Ittaphal	...	mut-te-li-du
Pael	... ul-lid	mul-li-du, mu-li-du
Iphtaal		mut-te-el-la-du
Shaphel	... su-lid	mu-sa-li-du, mus-te-li-du
Istaphal	... [su-te-lid]	mus-te-li-du

Verbs ו"פ.

KAL.

PERMANSIVE. Singular.	PRESENT. Singular.		AORIST. Singular.		IMPERATIVE AND PRECATIVE. Singular.	
1. [inikacu]		i-na-ak		i-ni-ik "*I suckled*"		li-nik
2. *Masc.* ...	" "	ti-na-ak	" "	ti-ni-ik	" "	nik
2. *Fem.* ...	" "	ti-na-ki	" "	ti-ni-ki	" "	ni-ki
3. *Masc.* ...	" "	i-nak	" "	i-nik	" "	li-nik
3. *Fem.* ...	" "	ti-nak	" "	ti-nik		...
Plural.	*Plural.*		*Plural.*		*Plural.*	
1.	" "	ni-nak	" "	ni-nik		...
2. *Masc.* ...	" "	ti-na-ku	" "	ti-ni-kn	" "	ni-kn
2. *Fem.* ...	" "	ti-na-ka	" "	ti-ni-ka	" "	ni-ka
3. *Masc.* [iniku]	" "	i-na-ku	" "	i-ni-ku	" "	li-ni-ku
3. *Fem.* ...	" "	i-na-ka	" "	i-ni-ka	" "	li-ni-ka

PARTICIPLE.

i-ni-ku

PARADIGM OF THE OTHER CONJUGATIONS.

PERMANSIVE.	PRESENT.		AORIST.	
Iphtcal ... [tennk]		i-ti-na-ak		i-ti-nik
Niphal ... [nenuk]	" "	i-ni-na-ak	" "	i-ni-nik
Ittaphal ...	" "	it-ti-nak	" "	it-ti-nik
Pael ... [cnnak]	" "	i-en-nak	" "	i-en-nik
	" "	in-nak	" "	in-nik
Iphtaal ...	" "	yut-te-en-nak	" "	yut-te-en-nik
Shaphel ... [senak]	" "	yu-se-nak	" "	yu-se-nik
Istaphal ... [satenak]	" "	yus-te-nak	" "	yus-te-nik
Istataphal ... [satetinak]		yus-te-te-nak	" "	yus-te-te-nik

IMPERATIVE.		PARTICIPLE.		
Iphteal	... [it-nik]	⟪cuneiform⟫		mu-ti-ni-ku
Niphal	... ni-nik	,,	,,	mu-ni-ni-ku
Ittaphal	[ni-ti-nik] ...	,,	,,	mu-te-ni-ku
Pael	un-nik "....	,,	,,	mu-en-ni-ku
Iphtaal	it-tin-nik ...	,,	,,	mut-te-en-ni-ku
Shaphel	su-nik ...	,,	,,	mu-se-ni-ku
Istaphal	... su-te-nik ...	,,	,,	mus-te-ni-ku
Istataphal	... [su-te-te-nik]	,,	,,	[mus-te-te-ni-ku]

N.B.—All these verbs are greatly confounded with one another, and had also a tendency to adopt forms borrowed from verbs ע״פ, consequently the same verb (e.g. *asabu*) might have some forms which presupposed a verb א׳ פ, others which presupposed a verb ו״פ (*usabu*), others which presupposed a verb י׳פ (*nasabu*), &c. Thus the precative *lusib*, *lusibu* given above comes not from *asabu* (verb א״פ), but from *usabu* (verb ו״פ).

Verbs ע"פ:—

KAL.

	PERMANSIVE.		PRESENT.
	Singular.		*Singular.*
1.	[epsacu]	𒀀𒉺𒀸	e-pa-as, ep-pas "*I make*"
2. *Masc.* ...	[epsat]	𒋫𒉺𒀸	te-pa-as, &c.
2. *Fem.* ...	—	„ „	te-pa-si
3. *Masc.* ...	e-pis	„ „	e-pa-as
3. *Fem.* ...	—	„ „	te-pa-as
	Plural.		*Plural.*
1. ...	—	𒉈𒉺𒀸	ne-pa-as
2. *Masc.* ...	—	„ „	te-pa-su
2. *Fem.* ...	—	„ „	te-pa-sa
3. *Masc.* ...	[e-pi-su]	„ „	e-pa-su
3. *Fem.* ... 𒀀𒉿𒊭	e-pi-sa	„ „	e-pa-sa
	Dual.		*Dual.*
3.	[episā]	„ „	[epasā]

	AORIST.			IMPERATIVE AND PRECATIVE.
	Singular.			*Singular.*
1. ... 𒀀𒄴	e-pus	𒀀 ✦	e-mid "*I stood*"	𒆠 𒄴 li-pus
2. *Masc.* ... „ „	te-pus	„	te-mid	„ „ e-pus
2. *Fem.* ... „ „	te-pu-si	„	te-mi-di	„ „ e-pu-si
3. *Masc.* ... „ „	e-pus	„	e-mid	„ „ li-pus
3. *Fem.* ... „ „	te-pus	„	te-mid	„ „ —
	Plural.			*Plural.*
1. ... „ „	ne-pus	„	ne-mid	„ „ —
2. *Masc.* ... „ „	te-pu-su	„	te-mi-du	„ „ e-pu-su
2. *Fem.* ... „ „	te-pu-sa	„	te-mi-da	„ „ e-pu-sa
3. *Masc.* ... „ „	e-pu-su	„	e-mi-du	„ „ li-pu-su
3. *Fem.* ... „ „	e-pu-sa	„	e-mi-da	„ „ li-pu-sa
	Dual.			
3. ... „ „	[epusā]	„	emidā]	

INFINITIVE.   𒀀𒉿𒌋 e-pi-su   𒀀𒉽𒌋 a-pū-su "*to make*" | PARTICIPLE.   𒀀𒉿𒌋 e-pi-su

	PERMANSIVE.			PRESENT.		AORIST.		
Iphteal ...	𒍦𒁹 𒐊	et-pus	𒐊𒁹 𒌑 𒌋 𒌋		e-tap-pas	𒐊𒁹 𒌋 𒐊		e-te-pus
Niphal ...	,, ,,	[nebus]	𒌋𒁹 𒌋 𒌋		ip-pas, i-pas	,,	,,	ip-pis, i-pis
Ittaphal...	,, ,,	[netepus]	𒍦𒁹 𒌋 𒌋 𒌋		it-te-pas	,,	,,	it-te-pis
Pael ...	,, ,,	[eppas]	𒌋 𒌋 𒌋		yup-pas	,,	,,	yup-pis
Iphtaal ...	,, ,,	—	𒐊𒌋 𒌋 𒌋𒁹 𒌋 𒌋		yu-te-ip-pas	,,	,,	yu-te-ip-pis
Shaphel ...	,, ,,	[sepas]	𒐊𒌋 𒌋 𒌋 𒌋		yu-se-pas	,,	,,	yu-se-pis
Istaphal...	,, ,,	[satepas]	𒁹 𒌋 𒌋 𒌋		yus-te-pas	,,	,,	yus-te-pis

	IMPERATIVE.				PARTICIPLE.	
Iphteal ...	𒍦𒁹 𒐊 𒌋𒁹	et-pis		𒌋 𒌋 𒐊 𒁹		mu-te-pi-su
Niphal ...	,, ,,	ni-ip-pis		𒌋 𒌋 𒐊 𒁹		mu-ne-pi-su
Ittaphal ...	,, ,,	ni-te-pis		𒌋 𒌋 𒌋 𒁹		mu-te-pa-su
Pael ...	𒐊𒌋 𒐊 𒌋𒁹	up-pis		𒌋 𒐊 𒐊 𒁹		mup-pi-su
Iphtaal ...	,, ,,	—		𒌋𒁹 𒌋 𒌋𒁹 𒐊 𒁹		mut-te-ip-pi-su
Shaphel ...	,, ,,	su-pis		𒌋 𒌋 𒐊 𒁹		mu-si-pi-su
Istaphal ...	,, ,,	su-ut-te-pis		𒐊𒌋 𒌋 𒐊 𒁹		mus-te-pi-su

The Babylonian dialect had 𒐊 𒐊𒁹 *i-bus* or 𒐊𒁹 𒐊 𒐊𒁹 *e-i-bus*, *i-bas* or *e-i-bas*, *i-bu-su* or *e-i-bu-su*, and *i-ba-su* or *e-i-ba-su*, instead of the 3rd pers. sing. and pl. forms given above. [A Babylonian *b* often represented an Assyrian *p*.] The Babylonian dialect also said 𒐊𒌋 𒐊𒌋 𒐊 𒌋 *yu-'ub-bas*, &c., instead of the contracted *yubbas*, &c.

CONCAVE VERBS.

KAL.

	PERMANSIVE. Singular.				PRESENT. Singular.	
1.		ca-ma-cu "*I rise*"			a-tar	
		ca'-a-na-cu, "*I establish*"			at-tar "*I bring back*"	
2. *Masc.*	,, ,,	[camat, ca'anat]		,, ,,	ta-tar, &c.	
2. *Fem.*	—	—		,, ,,	ta-ta-ri	
3. *Masc.*		ca-am		,, ,,	i-tar	
,,		ca-in		,, ,,	,,	
3. *Fem.*	,, ,,	[camat] [ca-i-nat]		,, ,,	ta-tar	

	Plural.				Plural.	
1.	—	—		,, ,,	na-tar	
2. *Masc.*	—	—		,, ,,	ta-ta-ru	
2. *Fem.*	—	—		,, ,,	ta-ta-ra	
3. *Masc.*		ca-mu, ca-i-nu		,, ,,	i-ta-ru	
3. *Fem.*	,, ,,	ca-ma, ca-i-na		,, ,,	i-ta-ra	

	Dual.				Dual.	
3.		camā		,, ,,	i-ta-ra-a	

	Singular.			AORIST.	Plural.	
1.		a-tur, at-tur		a-ciś "*I cut off*"	na-tur	na-ciś
2. *Masc.*	,,	ta-tur, &c.	,,	ta-ciś	,, ta-tu-ru	,, ta-ci-śu
2. *Fem.*	,,	ta-tu-ri	,,	ta-ci-śi	,, ta-tu-ra	,, ta-ci-śa
3. *Masc.*	,,	i-tur	,,	i-ciś	,, i-tu-ru	,, i-ci-śu
3. *Fem.*	,,	ta-tur	,,	ta-ciś	,, i-ta-ra	,, i-ci-śa

					Dual.	
3.	,,				i-tu-ra-a	,, i-ci-śa-a

IMPERATIVE AND PRECATIVE.

Singular.		Plural.
1. 𒀭 lu-ut-tur, lu-tur-ru		
2. *Masc.* tir, tir-ra 𒀭 tar		𒀭 du-ku "*smite ye*," cinu "*establish ye*"
𒀭 cin 𒀭 duk		
2. *Fem.* „ ti-ri, ta-ri, ci-ni, du-ci		„ du-cā, ci-nä
3. *M. and F.* „ lit-tur, li-tur		„ lit-tu-ru, li-tu-ru
		Dual.
		„ lit-tu-ra, li-tu-ra

INFINITIVE.

𒀭 ta'-a-ru *to turn*

PARTICIPLE ACT.

𒀭 ta'-i-ru   𒀭 ca'-i-nu

PARTICIPLE PASS.

𒀭 ti-ru   𒀭 di-ku   𒀭 ci-nu

PARADIGM OF THE OTHER CONJUGATIONS.

	PERMANSIVE.			PRESENT.	
Iphteal.	𒀭 𒀭 𒀭	{ te-bā-cu "*I come*" {[te-cin]	𒀭 𒀭	ic-ta-an	
			𒀭 𒀭	it-ba-a	
Niphalel …	„ „	[na-ac-nu-un]	„ „	ic-ca-na-an	
Ittaphalel …	„ „	[na-ac-te-nun]	„ „	it-tac-na-an	
Pael …	𒀭 𒀭 𒀭	ci-i-in	„ „	{ yu-uc-ca-an { yuc-ca-an	
Iphtael	„ „	—	„ „	yuc-ta-an	
Palel …	𒀭 𒀭	cu-un-nu, 3*rd pl.*	„ „	yuc-na-an	
Iphtalel	„ „	—	„ „	ic-te-na-an	
Shaphel …	„ „	[sa-ca-in]	„ „	yu-sa-ca-an	
Istaphal …	„ „	[sa-te-ca-an]	„ „	yus-ta-ca-an	
Aphel	„ „	—	„ „	yu-ca-(y)an	
Itaphal …	„ „	—	„ „	yuc-ca-an	
Shaphael …	„ „	[saccen]	„ „	yu-sac-ca-an	
Istaphael …	„ „	—	„ „	yus-tac-ca-an	
Shaphel Pass.	„ „	[su-cu-un]	𒀭	yu-su-ca-an	

PARADIGM OF THE OTHER CONJUGATIONS.

	AORIST.		IMPERATIVE.	PARTICIPLE.
Iphteal	[cuneiform] ic-ti-in / [cuneiform] it-bu'		[ci-tu-un] / [te-bu]	[cuneiform] mu-uc-ti-nu
Niphalel	,, ,,	{ ic-ca-nin / iz-za-nun }	na-ac-nin	,, ,, mu-uc-ca-ni-nu
Ittaphalel	,, ,,	it-tac-nin	ni-tac-nin	,, ,, mut-tac-na-nu
Pael	,, ,,	{ yu-uc-cin / yuc-cin }	[uc-cin]	,, ,, mu-uc-ci-nu
Iphteal	,, ,,	yuc-ti-in	—	,, ,, mu-tac-ci-nu
Palel	,, ,,	yuc-ni-in	uc-ni-in	,, ,, mu-uc-ti-nu
Iphtalel	,, ,,	ic-te-nin	—	,, ,, —
Shaphel	,, ,,	yu-sa-cin	su-cu-un	,, ,, mu-sa-ci-nu
Istaphel	,, ,,	yus-ta-cin	su-ut-cu-un	,, ,, mu-sac-ci-nu
Aphel	,, ,,	yu-cin	cin, cu-un	,, ,, mu-ci-nu
Itaphal	,, ,,	yuc-cin	—	,, ,, mu-uc-ci-nu
Shaphael	,, ,,	yu-sac-cin	su-uc-cu-un	,, ,, mu-sac-ci-nu
Istaphael	,, ,,	[yus-tac-cin]	—	,, ,, mus-tac-ci-nu
Shaphel Pass.	[cuneiform]	yu-su-cin	—	,, ,, —

It will be noticed that Palel and Iphtalel regularly appear in these Concave Verbs, and that Niphalel and Ittaphalel take the place of Niphal and Ittaphal.

The permansive of Pael changes *ayya* into *i*, and has a passive or neuter signification.

Verbs ל״א, ל״ה, ל״ו, ל״י, ל״ע.

KAL.

PERMANSIVE (or Perfect).		PRESENT.		AORIST.	
Singular.		*Singular.*		*Singular.*	
1.	𒈾-𒊓-𒀸 na-sa-cu "I lift up"	𒀀𒆗𒁉 a-gab-bi' "I speak"	𒀝𒁉 ag-bi'	𒀊𒉡 ab-nu' "I built"
2. *Masc.*	𒈾-𒊓-� na-sa-at ...	,, ,, ta-gab-bi'...	,, tag-bi'	,, tab-nu
2. *Fem.*	— — ...	,, ,, ta-gab-bi'	,, tag-bi'	,, tab-nu
3. *Masc.*	𒈾-𒋢 na-su ...	,, ,, i-gab-bi' ...	,, ig-bi'	,, ib-nu'
3. *Fem.*	𒈾-𒊓𒀜 na-sat ...	,, ,, ta-gab-bi'	,, tag-bi'	,, tab-nu'
Plural.		*Plural.*		*Plural.*	
1.	— — ...	,, ,, na-gab-bi'	,, nag-bi'	,, nab-nu
2. *Masc.*	— — ...	,, ,, ta-gab-bu	,, tag-bu	,, tab-nu
2. *Fem.*	— — ...	,, ,, ta-gab-ba	,, tag-ba	,, tab-na
3. *Masc.*	𒈾-𒋢-𒌋 na-su-u ...	,, ., i-gab-bu ...	,, ig-bu	,, ib-nu
3. *Fem.*	𒈾-𒊓-𒀀 na-sa-a ...	,, ,, i-gab-ba ...	,, ig-ba	,, ib-na
Dual.		*Dual.*		*Dual.*	
3.	𒈾-𒊓-𒀀 na-sa-a ...	,, ,, i-gab-ba-a	,, ig-ba-a	,, ib-na-a

IMPERATIVE AND PRECATIVE.				INFINITIVE.	
Singular.					
1.	𒇻𒊌𒁉 lu-ug-bi'	𒇻𒌈𒉡 lu-ub-nu'		𒁀𒉡 ba-nu "to build"
2. *Masc.*	,, ba-ni, ba-an	,, ,, khi-dhi'		�ga-a-bu ga-a-bu "to speak"
2. *Fem.*	,, ba-ni-i	,, ,, khi-dhi-i		𒈾𒀀𒋢 na-a-su "to lift"
3. *Masc.*	,, li-ig-bi'	,, , li-ib-nu'		
Plural.				PARTICIPLE.	
2. *Masc.*	,, ba-nu-u			𒁀𒉡 ba-nu	
2. *Fem.*	,, ba-na-a			� ga-bu	
3. *Masc.*	,, li-ib-nu-u				
3. *Fem.*	,, lib-na-a				

Verbs ᵧ″ᒇ properly have *e* in the last syllable, as ⊨⟨𝕀𝕀 𝕀⊢ ⊨𝕀𝕀 *is-me-e* "he heard," but *i* frequently takes its place. In the plural we may have ⊨⟨𝕀𝕀 𝕀⊢ ⟨ *is-me-u* as well as ⊨⟨𝕀𝕀 ⭙⭣ *is-mu*.

PARADIGM OF THE OTHER CONJUGATIONS.

	PERMANSIVE.		PRESENT.
Iphteal ...	[kitbu']	▸⟨𝕀⭤ ⭙𝕀 ⊒𝕀	ik-te-ba'
Pael	[kabba']	,, ,,	yu-kab-ba'
Iphtaal ...	—	,, ,,	yuk-tâb-ba'
Niphal ...	▸⊞ ⭙⭣ nak-bu'	,, ,,	ik-ka-ba'
Ittaphal ... ,, ,,	[nak-te-bu']	,, ,,	it-tak-ba'
Niphael ... ,, ,,	[nakabbu']	,, ,,	it-kab-ba'
Shaphel ... ,, ,,	[sakba']	,, ,,	yu-sak-ba'
Istaphal ... ,, ,,	[satkeba']	,, ,,	yus-te-ik-ba'
Shaphael ... ,, ,,	[sakabba']	,, ,,	yus-kab-ba'
Istaphael ... ,, ,,	[satkabba']	,, ,,	yus-kab-ba'
Shaphel Pass... ⊨⊐ ⊨𝔣⊨ ⭙⭣ ku-ub-bu'		,, ,,	yu-kù-ub-ba'

	AORIST.		IMPERATIVE.
Iphteal ...	▸⟨𝕀⭤ ⭙𝕀 ⊐ ik-te-bi'	⊨𝕀𝕀 ⊐	kit-bi'
Pael	,, ,, yu-kab-bi'	,, ,,	ku-ub-bi'
Iphtaal ...	,, ,, yuk-tab-bi'	,, ,,	ki-tib-bi'
Niphal ...	,, ,, ik-ka-bi'	,, ,,	nak-bi'
Ittaphal ...	,, ,, it-tak-bi'	,, ,,	ni-tak-bi'
Niphael ...	,, ,, ik-kab-bi'	,, ,,	[na-kab-bi']
Shaphel ...	,, ,, yu-sak-bi'	,, ,,	suk-bu'
Istaphal ...	,, ,, yus-te-ik-bi'	,, ,,	su-te-ik-bi'
Shaphael ...	,, ,, yus-kab-bi'	,, ,,	[su-ku-ub-bu']
Istaphael ...	,, ,, yus-kab-bi'	,, ,,	[su-te-ku-ub-bi']
Shaphel Pass...	,, ,, yu-ku-ub-bi'		—

PARTICIPLE.

Iphteal...	▸⊐ ⭙𝕀 ⭙⭣⊢ ⟨ muk-te-bu-u		*Niphael*...	▸⊒ 𝕀⟨𝕀⟨𝕀 ⭙⭣⊢ ⟨ muk-kab-bu-u	
Pael ...	,, ,, mu-kab-bu-u		*Shaphel*...	,, ,, mu-sak-bu-u	
Iphtaal	,, ,, muk-tab-bu-u		*Istaphal*	,, ,, mus-te-ik-bu-u	
Niphal...	,, ,, muk-ka-bu-u		*Shaphael*	,, ,, mus-kab-bu-u	
Ittaphal	,, ,, mut-tak-bu-u		*Istaphael*	,, ,, mus-te-kab-bu-u	

By combining the forms given in these Paradigms the student will be able to obtain the forms of *doubly defective Verbs* like 𒀀𒋫𒌅 *atsu* "to go forth," 𒆷𒌑 *lavu* "to cling to," 𒁀𒌑 *bavu* "to come,"

PARADIGM OF QUADRILITERAL VERBS.

The Characters to be added by the Student.

	PERMANSIVE.					PRESENT.
Kal (=Palel) ...	𒀀𒋫𒌅	pal-cit				{ i-pal-cat "*he crosses*" iš-khu-par "*he overthrows*" }
Iphtalel	,,	,,	[pitlucut]	𒀀𒋫𒌅		yup-tal-cat
Saphalel	,,	,,	[saplacat]	,,	,,	yus-pal-cat
Istaphalel	,,	,,	[saptelcat]	,,	,,	yus-ta-pal-cat
Niphalel	,,	,,	[naplacut]	,,	,,	ip-pal-cat
Ittaphalel	,,	,,	[naptelcut]	,,	,,	it-ta-pal-cat
Niphalla	,,	,,	—	,,	,,	ip-pal-ca-ta-at

	AORIST.		IMPERATIVE.	PARTICIPLE.
Kal (=*Palel*)	{ i-pal-cit, i-pa-la-cit ip-la-cit, iš-khu-pir }		pal-cit	mu-pal-ci-tu
Iphtalel ...	yup-tal-cit		pi-tal-cat	mu-up-tal-ci-tu
Saphalel ...	yus-pal-cit		su-pal-cut	mu-pal-ci-tu
Istaphalel ...	yus-ta-pal-cit		sit-pal-cut	mus-ta-pal-ci-tu
Niphalel ...	{ ip-pal-cit ip-par-sud "*he pur-sued*" }		ni-pal-cat	mu-up-pal-ci-tu
Ittaphalel ...	it-ta-pal-cit		[na-te-pal-cat]	mut-ta-pal-ci-tu
Niphalla ...	𒀀𒋫𒌅 ip-pal-cit-it		... ...	mu-up-pal-cit-tu

VERBS TO BE CONJUGATED BY THE STUDENT.

1.	ca-sa-du	to obtain	21.		to extend
2.	na-ba-lu	to fall, destroy	22.		to proclaim
3.	pa-ra-tsu	to speak falsely	23.		to cut off
4.	tsa-ba-tu	to take	24.		to slay
5.	sa-dha-ru	to write	25.		to oversee
6.	sa-pa-ru	to send	26.		to make bricks
7.	ma'-a-tu	to die	27.		to thresh
8.	sa-la-dhu	to rule	28.		to measure
9.	ba-kha-ru	to choose	29.		to pour
10.	na-ca-ru	to be strange			

Verbs to be transliterated and conjugated by the Student.

11.	to protect
12.	to complete
13.	to collect
14.	to finish
15.	to hear
16.	to trust
17.	to destroy
18.	to cross over
19.	to curse
20.	to ask

Verbs to be conjugated and the Characters added by the Student.

30.	ca-ra-bu	to be near
31.	ka-a-su	to snare
32.	e-bi-lu	to be lord
33.	ha-pa-cu	to smite
34.	ma-la-cu	to rule
35.	ca-na-su	to submit
36.	ma-kha-ru	to be present, to receive
37.	sa-ra-cu	to deliver
38.	na-du-u	to place
39.	za-ca-ru	to remember
40.	a-ba-lu	to bring

Verbs *to be conjugated and the Characters added by the Student.*

41.	e-ri-bu ...	*to descend*	59.		e-zi-bu ...	*to forsake*
42.	e-lu-u ...	*to ascend*	60.		pa-ta-khu	*to cut open*
43.	e-ci-mu...	*to strip, to take*	61.		ga-ru-u ...	*to war*
44.	sa-la-lu ...	*to spoil*	62.		sa-ca-ru...	*to drink*
45.	khar-pa-su	*to be violent*	63.		ra-tsa-pu	*to build*
46.	ca-vu-u ...	*to burn*	64.			*to build*
47.	sa-tu-u ...	*to drink*	65.			*to go*
48.	sa-la-pu...	*to pull out*	66.			*to hate*
49.	ka-lu-u ...	*to burn*	67.			*to see*
50.	na-ca-ru	*to dig*	68.			*to fill*
51.	ma-lu-u...	*to fill*	69.			*to die*
52.	śa-kha-ru	*to go round*	70.			*to assemble*
53.	e-ni-khu	*to decay*	71.			*to burn*
54.	pa-ra-ru	*to crush*	72.			*to learn*
55.	kha-ba-tu	*to devastate*	73.			*to make*
56.	par-sa-du	*to fly*	74.			*to conquer*
57.	ta-ra-tsu	*to arrange*	75.			*to be good*
58.	na-pa-ra-cu	*to break*				

LIST OF ASSYRIAN PREPOSITIONS.

No.	Cuneiform	Transliteration	Meaning	No.	Cuneiform	Transliteration	Meaning
1.	𒀠 𒀝, 𒀠	a-di ...	*up to*	18.	𒅎	im ...	*from, with*
2.	𒀠 𒀭	a-khi, a-kha-at	*at the side of*	19.	𒀸 𒈾, 𒉌	ina, in ...	*in, by, with*
3.	𒀠 𒀴	a-khar ...	*behind*	20.	𒅔 𒈾	in-na, in-nannu	*in, from*
4.	𒀠 𒈾, 𒀭	a-na, an	*to, for*	21.	𒀼 𒊺	it-ti, it...	*with, during*
5.	𒅈 𒋢	ar-cu, ar-ci	*after*	22.	𒆠	ci ...	*according to, as*
6.	𒀸 𒋢	as-su, as-sum	*in, by, in regard to*	23.	𒆠 𒈠	ci-ma, cim	*like*
7.	𒁀 𒇻	ba-lu, baliv	*without*	24.	𒆠 𒁉	ci-bit ...	*by command of*
8.	𒁉 𒆳	bi-rid ...	*within, near*	25.	𒆠 𒆠	ci-rib ...	*in the midst of*
9.	𒁲 𒆠	di-khi ...	*opposite*	26.	�- 𒌝	cu-um ...	*instead of*
10.	𒌌 𒇷	ul-li ...	*among*	27.	𒆷 𒉺 𒉌	la-pa-ni...	*before*
11.	𒌌 𒇷 𒈾	ul-lā-nu	*before*	28.	𒇻 𒈨 𒋾 𒇷	li-me-ti, li	*near*
12.	𒌌 𒇷 𒉏 𒈠	ul-la-num-ma	*upon*	29.	𒇺 𒁉	lib-bi, libba	*in the midst of*
13.	𒌌 𒌈	ul-tu ...	*from, out of*	30.	𒈠 𒄴 𒊑	makh-ri ...	*before*
14.	𒅖 𒌈	is-tu ...	*from, out of*	31.	𒈪 𒄴 𒊑	mi-ikh-rit	*among*
15.	𒅋 𒆷 𒈬	il-la-mu...	*before*	32.	𒉪	nir ...	*below, near, against*
16.	𒅋 𒆷 𒀭	il-la-an [*or* elan]	*beyond*	33.	𒉈 𒈪 𒁺	ne-mi-du	*towards*
17.	𒅋 𒇻	il-lu ...	*upon*	34.	𒅆 𒄴 𒋾	śi-khar-ti	*throughout*
				35.	𒂊 𒆷	e-la ...	*over*

ASSYRIAN PREPOSITIONS—*continued.*

36.	[illegible]	e-la-at ...	*except*
37.	[illegible], [illegible]	e-li, el ...	*over, upon, above, beside*
38.	[illegible]	ė-la-an ...	*beyond*
39	[illegible]	e-ma ...	*around*
40.	[illegible], [illegible]	er-ti ...	*against*
41.	[illegible], [illegible]	pa-ni, pan	*before*
42.	[illegible]	tsir ...	*against, upon*
43.	[illegible]	sa ...	*of, in regard to*
44.	[illegible]	sap-tu ...	*by the help of*
45.	[illegible]	se-pu ...	*under*
46.	[illegible]	tic ...	*behind*

THE COMPOUND PREPOSITIONS.

1.	𒀀 𒈾 𒀉 𒋾	a-na it-ti	*to be with*
2.		a-na la	*not to be*
3.		a-na im	*to*
4.		a-na e-li	*over*
5.		a-na er-ti	*to the presence of*
6.		ul-tu ci-rib	*from the midst of*
7.		ul-tu lib-bi	*from the midst of*
8.		ul-tu pa-ni	*from before*
9.		i-na bi-bil, i-na bi-ib-lat	*in the midst of*
10.		i-na a-di dhe-mi	*by command of*
11.		i-na ci-rib	*in the midst of*
12.		i-na lib-bi	*in the midst of*
13.		i-na śu-ki	*in front of*
14.		i-na ni-rib	*near to*
15.		i-na la	*for want of*
16.		i-na pan	*from before*
17.		i-na e-li	*above*
18.		i-na er-ti	*after*
19.		i-na tir-tsi, i-na tar-tsi	*in the* { *presence* / *time* } *of*
20.		i-na an-ni	*at this time*
21.		ci la	*without*
		&c., &c.	

THE CONJUNCTIONS.

1. 𒀭 *or* 𒈾	u *or* vā	*and* (between nouns and clauses)	12.		ma-a ...	*that, for* umma (see Adverbs)
𒂊	vă ...	*and* (after verbs)	13.		sa ...	*when, because, where, that*
2. 𒀭, 𒂊	û ...	*or*	14.		sum-ma	*if, thus, when*
3.	ai ...	*not* (with the Imperat. or Precat.)	15.		al-la sa	*after that*
4.	ac-ca	*how ?*	16.		a-di-sa, a-di e-li sa	*in so far as, while*
5.	im ...	*if*				
6.	as-su	*when, meanwhile, now*	17.		ar-ci sa	*after that*
7.	i-nu...	*behold, now*	18.		im ma-ti-ma	*if at all*
8.	cī ...	*when, thus, as, while*	19.		i-na ma-ti-ma	*in any case*
9.	ci-ma	*as, thus*				
10.	lā ...	*not*	20.		ci-sa ...	*whenever*
	ul ...	*not* (with verbs)	21.		lib-bu sa	*just as*
11.	lū ...	*whether, or, truly* (verbal prefix of past time)	22.		sa ma-ti-ma	*of what place ?*

THE ADVERBS.

The most common mode of forming the adverb in Assyrian was by attaching the termination *-is* to the construct-state of a noun (whether sing. or pl.); as *rab-is* "greatly," *el-is* "above," *sallat-is* "for a spoil," *caccab-is* "like a star," *sadan-is* "like mountains." The accusative case of the noun, with or without the mimmation, might also be used adverbially, as *palcā* "amply," *rubam* "greatly."

The genitive also, with or without the mimmation, is sometimes found; as *batstsi* "in ruin," *labirim* "of old."

The most common adverbs of place and time are the following:—

1.	𒀀𒃶𒈾 a-gan-na ...	*here*		11.	ci-ha-am ...	*thus*
2.	a-di ...	*till*		12.	lu-ma(h)-du	*much*
3.	ai-um-ma, ya-um-ma, um-ma	*never*		13.	makh-ri ...	*formerly*
	.... ►𒂍 .... la			14.	ma-te-ma...	*in times past*
				15.	e-nin-na ...	*again*
4.	al-lu, al-la, al-la sa	*then, afterwards*		16.	e-nu-va ...	*when, at that time*
5.	ar-ci ...	*afterwards*		17.	pa-na-ma...	*formerly*
6.	u-di-na ...	*at the same [time]*		18.	tsa-tis ...	*in future*
				19.	sa... ...	*when*
7.	um-ma ...	*thus, that*		20.	sa-num-ma, sa-nam-ma	*in a foreign land, elsewhere*
8.	ul-lā-na, ultu ulla	*from that time, from of old*				
				21.	ina yumi suma	*at that time*
9.	zi-is ...	*as of old*				
10.	ca-la-ma ...	*of all kinds*		22.	um-maas-su	*because*

DERIVATION OF NOUNS.

A large proportion of Assyrian nouns are derived from different forms of the verb. Thus from Kal we have the infinitives ⬛⬛⬛ *ra-kha-a-tsu* "to inundate," ⬛⬛⬛ *ni-ci-i-śu* "to cut off," and ⬛⬛⬛ *su-mu-u-ru* "to keep;" the participle passive ⬛⬛⬛ *da-li-i-khu* "troubled," and the active participle ⬛⬛⬛ *ma-a-li-cu* "ruling" where the long *ā* of the first syllable serves to distinguish it from *mă-li-cu* "a king," which is derived from the Permansive.

From Pael we have nouns like ⬛⬛⬛ *kar-ra-du* "war-like," *lim-mu-nu* "injured."

From Palel, ⬛⬛⬛ *nam-ri-ri* "bright."

From Iphteal and Iphtaal, ⬛⬛⬛ *cit-ru-bu* "a meeting," *lat-bu-su* "clothed," *git-ma-lu* "a benefactor."

From Shaphel, ⬛⬛⬛ *sap-sa-ku* "an opening," *sum-cu-tu* "a slaughter."

From Niphal, ⬛⬛⬛ *nab-kha-ru* "collected," *nab-ni-tu* "offspring," *num-kha-ru* "a receipt."

From the weak verbs come words like ⬛⬛⬛ *mi-ru* "offspring" for *ma'-iru*, *sa-hu* "summit" from *nasu*, and from verbs ץ"פ, *lit-tu* (for *lid-tu*), *li-du*, *li-i-tu*, *li-da-a-tu*, and *lit-tu-tu*, all meaning "offspring." Also forms which repeat the second radical, as *li-lic-cu* "a going," *lil-li-du* "a birth," *dadmu* "man," the Heb. *adam* אדם.

When a monosyllable is repeated the last consonant of the first syllable is generally assimilated to the first consonant of the second syllable, as ⬛⬛⬛ *kak-ka-du* (for *kad-kadu*) "a head," *ca-ac-ca-bu* (for *cab-cabu*) "a star."

The prefix *M* denotes the instrument, action, or place, as ⬛⬛⬛ *man-za-zu* a "bulwark."

The prefix *T* (another form of Iphteal) builds abstracts, as ⬛⬛⬛ *tas-me-a-tu* "a hearing," *te-ni-se-tu* "mankind," *tu-ku-ma-tu* or *tuk-ma-tu* "opposition." Also adjectives as *Tas-me-tu* "she who hears" (the wife of Nebo).

Roots may be increased by prefixing a vowel, as ⬛⬛⬛ *al-ca-cat* or *il-ca-cat* " stories," *e-da-khu* " warrior," *im-mi-ru* " youngling," *u-ta-a-ma* "lawgiver."

A word might be lengthened by affixing *ānu* (also *īnu* or *innu* and *ūnu*) to the construct; ⸢cuneiform⸣ *cir-ba-a-nu* " an offering," ⸢cuneiform⸣ *sil-dha-a-nu* "a king," ⸢cuneiform⸣ *te-er-din-nu* " a descent," ⸢cuneiform⸣ *a-gu-nu* " a crown." Words so formed were collectives.

Gentile nouns were formed by the termination *ai* (fem. *aitu*), as ⸢cuneiform⸣ ⸢cuneiform⸣ *ti-(h)am-ta-ai* " a sailor," ⸢cuneiform⸣ *Ba-bi-la-ai* " a Babylonian," *Dur-Sar-ci-na-ai-ti* " she of Dur-Sargon."

Quadriliterals are occasionally found, as well as quinqueliterals, as *a-sa-ri-du* "first-born," *khar-pa-su* " vehemence," *kha-mi-luhk-khi* " stores," *kha-ba-tsi-il-la-tu* " a lily."

Many Assyrian words are borrowed from Accadian.

PHONOLOGY.

The chief phonetic rules to be remembered are the following :—

1. A sibilant before a dental generally becomes *l*, as *kha-mil-tu* " five " for *kha-mis-tu*.

2. A dental followed by *s* is (together with the sibilant) resolved into *ss* or *s*, as ⸢cuneiform⸣ *ka-as-su* or ⸢cuneiform⸣ *ka-su* for *kat-su* " his hand."

3. A dental preceded by a sibilant is assimilated to the latter, and when the sibilant is *s* the last rule takes effect, as *its-tsa-bat* for *its-ta-bat* " he is taken," *is-sa-can* and *i-sa-can* for *is-ta-can* " he dwells."

4. After a guttural, the *t* of the secondary conjugations may change to *d* or *dh*, as *ik-dha-rib* for *ik-ta-rib* " he approached."

5. *Kh* in the other Semitic idioms, is frequently replaced in Assyrian by *h*, or lost altogether.

6. Instead of *k* the Babylonian dialect often has *g*, as *ga-tu* for *ka-tu* " hand ;" and this change of letter sometimes makes its way into the Assyrian dialect.

7. *C* frequently takes the place of *k* (especially at the beginning of a word), and also (but more rarely) of *g*, as ⟨𒂍⟩ ⟶𒉌 ⟶ *ci-ri-bu* for 𒂍 ⟶𒉌 ⟶ *ki-ri-bu* " neighbourhood," ⟨𒂍⟩ 𒉌 *ci-bit* for 𒂍 𒉌 *ki-bit* " command ;" and where the other Semitic dialects prefer the softer consonants (*g*, *z*), Assyrian often combines *c* and *ts* in a root.

8. *N* is generally assimilated to the following consonant, as *id-din* for *in-din* " he gave." Conversely, a double dental may be resolved into *nd* or *nt*.

9. *M* may become *n* before a dental, sibilant, or guttural, as *khan-sa* for *kham-sa* "five," and then be assimilated to the following consonant, as 𒀸 𒉌 𒀸 *ikhkhar* for *imkhar* "it is present." Conversely, double *b* or double *p* may be resolved into *mb* or *mp*, as *i-nam-bu'* for *i-nab-bu'* " he proclaims."

10. *E* (𒂊) is always a vowel, and is very frequently used as interchangeable with *i*.

N.B.—The Assyrians had considerable difficulty in adapting the characters of a foreign (Accadian) syllabary to express the sounds of their own language. Hence in the 3rd pers. sing. of a verb, whenever the form requires a prefixed *u* (in Pael, &c.), we have to supply a *y ;* thus 𒅥 must be read *yus*, not *us*, 𒅥 *yu*, not *u*. Before 𒅋, *h* has often to be understood, and sometimes has to be supplied (though not written) after a vowel. *M* and *v* were interchangeable in Accadian, and possibly also in Assyrian ; at all events they are interchangeable in the writing, and 𒈠, e.g., must sometimes be read *ma* and sometimes *va*, 𒀀 sometimes *am* and sometimes *av*. The chief drawback occasioned by the syllabary was that a final guttural may be read *g*, *c*, or *k*, a final dental *d*, *dh*, or *t*, a final labial *b* or *p*, a final sibilant *s* or *ś*, and even *z* or *ts*. Thus 𒁶 may be either *tig*, *tic*, or *tik*. Again, 𒅋 represented both *za* and *tsa*, 𒁕 *da* or *dha*, ⟨𒁲⟩ *di* or *dhi*, and 𒁍 *bu* or *pu*. Only a certain number of characters contained the vowel *e*. There was no *sh* or *th*.

READING LESSONS.

Extract from the Annals of TIGLATH-PILESER I (W.A.I. XVI, col. 8, line 39) :—

(39.) 𒀯𒀯 𒀯𒀯 𒀯𒀯 𒀯𒀯 𒀯𒀯 𒀯𒀯 𒀯𒀯 𒀯𒀯

li - ta - at   kur di - ya   ir - nin - tu   (40.) tam - kha - ri - ya

The records   *of my warriors,*   *the battle-shout*   *of my fighting,*

suc - nu - us   naciri   (41.) tsa - ê - ru - ut   D.P. A - sur   sa   D.P. A - nu   va

the submission of enemies   *hostile to*   *Asshur,*   *whom*   *Anu*   *and*

D.P. Rammânu   (42.) a - na   si - tsu - ti   is - ru - cu - u - ni

Rimmon   *to*   *destruction*   *have*   *given,*

(43.) i - na   D.P. na - ra a - ya   va   tim - me - ni - ya   (44.) al - dhu - ur

on   *my tablet*   *and*   *my foundation-stone*   *I wrote;*

i - na   bit D.P. A - nuv   va   D.P. Rammânu   (45.) ili   rabi

in the temple of Anu   *and*   *Rimmon,*   *the gods*   *great,*

beli - ya   (46.) a - na   tsa - at   yumi   as - cu - un   (47.) va

my lords,   *for*   *future*   *days*   *I established;*   *and*

D.P. na - ra - a - T   sa D.P. Sam - si D.P. Rammânu   (48.) a - bi - ya   a - ni - mis

the tablets   *of*   *Samas-Rimmon*   *my father*   *duly*

ab - su - us   D.P. niki   (49.) ak - ki   a - na   as - ri - su - nu   u - tir

I cleaned :   *victims*   *I sacrificed :*   *to*   *their places*   *I restored (them)*

(50.) a - na — ar - cat — yumi — a - na — YU- um — tsa- a - te — (51.) a - na
for — future — days, — for — a day — long hereafter, — for

ma - te - ma — ruba — ARC - u — (52.) e - nu - ma — bit — D.P. A - nuv — va
whatsoever — prince — hereafter (reigns). — When — the temple — of — Anu — and

D.P. Rammânu — ili — (53.) RABU - te — beli - ya — va — si - gur- ra -a- tu
Rimmon, the gods — great, — my lords, — and — the towers

54.) sa - ti - na — yu - sal- ba - ru - va — (55.) e - na - khu — an - khu - su -nu
these — grow old, and — decay, — their ruins

lu -ud-dis — (56.) D.P. na - ra - a - TI - ya — va — tim -me- ni - ya — (57.) ni -mes
may he renew, — my — tablets — and my foundation-stones — duly

li - ib- su- us — D.P. niki — lik - ki — (58.) a - na — as - ri - su -nu
may he cleanse, — victims — may he slay, — to — their places

lu - u - tir — (59.) va — sum - su — it - ti - ya — lil - dhu - ur
may he restore, — and his name — with mine — may he write.

(60.) ci -ma — ya- ti -ma — D.P. A- nuv — va — D.P. Rammânu — (61.) ili — rabi
Like — myself, — may Anu — and — Rimmon, — the great gods,

i - na — dhu - ub — lib - bi — (62.) va — ca - sad — ir - nin- te — dha - bis
in — soundness — of heart — and — conquest — in battle — bountifully

lidh -dhar- ru - su — (63.) sa — D.P. na - ra - a - TI - ya — va — tim -me- ni - ya
keep him. — He who — my inscriptions — and — my foundation-stones

(64.) i - khab - bu - u   i - śa - pa - nu
      shall conceal,   *shall hide,*

(65.) a - na   me   i - na - du - u
      to   the water   shall lay,

(66.) i - na   isati   i - kal - lu - u
      with   fire   shall burn,

(67.) i - na   epiri
      in   dust

i - ca - ta - mu   i - na   bit   cummi (?)
shall cover,   *in a house underground (?)*

(68.) a - sar   la - a - ma - ri
      a place   not seen

pi - si - ris   i - na - ci - mu
for interpretation   shall set,

(69.) sum sadh - ra   i - pa - si - dhu - va
      the name written   shall erase, and

(70.) sum - su   i - sa - dha - ru   va   mi - lim - ma
      his own name   shall write;   and   an attack

(71.) lim - na
      evil

i - kha - śa - śa - va
shall devise, and

(72.) a - na   pa - an   D.P.   na - ra - a - TI - ya
      against   the face   of   my inscriptions

(73.) yu - sap - ra - cu
      shall cause to break,

(74.) D.P. A - nu   va   D.P. Assuru   ili   rabi
      may   Anu   and   Assur, the gods great,

beli - ya
my lords,

(75.) iz - zi - is   li - cal - mu - su - va
      strongly   injure   him,   and

(76.) ar - ra - ta   ma - ru - us -, ta   li - ru - ru - su
      (with)   a   curse   grievous   may they curse him;

(77.) śarru - śu
      his kingdom

lis - ci - bu
may they dissipate,

(78.) sul   cuśśi   śar(u) - ti - su   li - śu - khu
      the ascent   of the throne   of his kingdom   may they remove

(79.) 𒀸 𒅁 𒁁 𒌑 𒂍 [𒈠] 𒋗 𒂍
tsab - hi   bilu - ti - su   lu - bal - lu
the armies   *of his lordship*   *may they devour,*

(80.) 𒂍 𒂍 𒅗 𒂍
cacci - su
his weapons

𒂍 𒄩 𒁁 𒐼 𒌋
lu - sab - bi - ru
may they break,

(81.) 𒉿 𒁁 𒅗 𒅗 𒂍 𒂍 𒄰 𒂍 𒅅 𒐕 𒌋
a - bi - ic - ti   um - ma - ni - su   lis - cu - nu
the destruction   *of his army*   *may they cause;*

(82.) 𒂍 𒀹 𒅗 𒀹 𒀀 𒈨 𒂍 𒌋 𒐼
i - na   pa - an   naciri - su   ca - nis
in the   *presence*   *of his enemies*   *wholly*

(83.) 𒂍 𒀸 𒅗 𒀸 𒂍
lu - se - si - bu - su
may they cause him to dwell;

𒀹 𒄷 𒂍 𒅗 𒅗 𒐼
D.P. Rammânu i - na   simmi
may the Air-god with   *pestilence*

(84.) 𒅗 𒂍 𒆗 𒀹 𒅅 𒀹 𒌋 𒐕
khul - te mat - su   li - ib - tsu
destructive his land   *cut off;*

(85.) 𒅅 𒐼 𒀹 𒅁 𒀹 𒐼𒐕 𒌋 𒅗𒐼𒐼 𒐊
su - un - ka   pu - pu - ta   khu - sakh - khu
want   *of crops,*   *famine,   (and)*

(86.) 𒀸 𒐊 𒉿 𒀹
pagri a - na
corpses against

𒀹 𒅗 𒂍 𒄫 𒅗
mat - ti - su   lid - di'
his land   *may he lay;*

(87.) 𒀸 𒌑 𒀹 𒂍 𒂍 𒉿 𒅗 𒂍 𒅗 𒐼
ana bil - ut   ma - la - a - ti - su   lik - bi'
against the sovereignty of his full-power   may he speak:

(88.) 𒀹 𒂍 𒅅 𒂍 𒀹 𒀹 𒂍 𒀹 𒅗 𒅗
sum - su   zir - su   ina mati   lu - khal - li - ik
his name,   *his seed*   *in the land*   *may he destroy.*

ANALYSIS.

39. *lītat*, pl. fem., construct form.

kurdi, for *kurădi*, pl. of *kuradu* " warrior ;" perhaps Ar. جدير.

ya, poss. pron., first person suffix.

irnintu, with vowel prefix, from רנן " to shout for joy."

40. *tamkhari*, gen. sing., Tiphel derivative from מהר " to be present," facing ;" hence " opposition " or " fighting."

sucnus, sing. construct, Shaphel passive deriv. from כבש " to subject."

náciri, masc. pl. gen., Kal participle of נכר, the Kal of which is not used in Hebrew.

41. *tsa'erut*, masc. pl., construct of the Kal part., *tsa'iru* " enemy," Heb. צר. The plural is also found under the forms *tsa'eri, tsa'iri, tsahri* and *tsayári*. E is incorrectly written for '*i*, which stands for *vi*.

Anu was originally the sky, *Rimmon* was the air-god.

42. *sitsuti*, sing. gen. fem. verbal noun. Aram. שצא, Targ. שצו " to destroy."

isrucūni, third pl. masc. perf., Kal of *saracu*.

43. *narā* (preceded by D.P. of " stone " *abnu*), apparently borrowed from Accadian. *Narā* (or *narū*) is fem., with pl. *narāti*.

timmeni, pl. masc., borrowed from Accadian.

44. *aldhur* for *asdhur*, 1st pers. sing. aor. Kal of שטר " to write."

bīt (for *bayit*), sing. construct ; Heb. בית.

45. *ili*, pl. masc. of '*ilu*; Heb. אל.

rabi, also *rabuti*, masc. pl., adj. ; Heb. רב.

bili or *beli*, pl. masc. of *belu*, Heb. בעל.

46. *tsāt*, fem. pl. construct ; abstract noun from יצא (Ass. *atsu*) " to go forth " (literally " the goings forth," " that which will go forth ").

yumi, pl. masc. of *yumu*, Heb. יום.

ascun, 1st pers. sing. aor. Kal of שכן (originally Shaphel of כון).

48. *'abi*, gen. sing. masc. of *abu* (אַב).

'*animes*, adverb in -*is* formed from pl. of *'anu*, "suitably, fitly." Cp. Ar. اَلِّي

absus, 1st per. sing. aor. Kal of בשש "to cleanse."

niki, pl. of *niku* "offering," "sacrifice;" Heb. נְקֵה.

49. *akki*; 1st pers. sing. aor. Kal of נקה (*naku'u*), from which *niku* is derived.

'*asri*, pl. of *'asru*, "a place;" Aram. (& Ar.) אתר.

utir, 1st pers. sing. aor. Aphel of *tāru*, "to come back," become," "be;" Heb. תור "to go about."

50. *'arcāt*, pl. fem. construct of an abstract *'arcu* for *aricu*, "after" p. ארך.

yum tsāte literally "day of the future;" *yum* in construct sing., *tsāte* abstract fem. pl.

51. *matema* "at any time," "at any place;" Cp. Heb. מתי "when."

rubu, from רב, literally "a great one."

52. *enuma*, adverb compounded of *enu* (Ar. عِنْدَ), and the pron. *ma* "that."

53. *sigurrātu*, pl. fem. of *sigurrătu*, "a closed place," hence "a temple-tower" or observatory, from סגר. It is written *ziggurrătu* in the Babylonian dialect.

54. *sātina*, pl. fem. of the pron. *su'atu*, *sātu*, agreeing with *sigurrātu*.

yusalbaru-va, 3rd pers. masc. aor. Shaphel of *labaru* "to be old," with the enclitic conjunction *va* (!) "and."

55. *enakhu*, 3rd. pers. masc. pl. aor. Kal of ענח.

'*ankhusunu*, for *ankhut-sunu*, *t* + *s* being replaced not only by *t* + *s̓*, but also by *s̓* alone.

ankhut is pl. masc. from *'ankhu* a subst. derived from ענח, *'ayin* becoming *'a*.

luddis, 3rd sing. masc. Precative Aphel of *hadasu* "to be new." Cp. Heb. הדש.

57. *nimes* for *'animes*, as in line 48. Verbs פ"נ drop their initial radical in many forms. (See my *Assyrian Grammar*, p. 108).

libsus, 3rd masc. sing. prec. Kal from *basasu* (as above).

likki', 3rd masc. sing. prec. Kal from *niku'u* (as above), the nasal being assimilated to the following letter.

58. *lutir*, 3rd masc. sing. prec. Aphel of *tāru* (as above).

9

59. *sum*, sing. masc. construct of *sumu* "a name ;" Heb. שֵׁם.

    itti, preposition ; Heb. אֵת.

    lildhur, 3rd masc. sing. prec. Kal of *sadharu* (as above).

60. *yatima*, 1st pers. pron., compounded of *ya* "I," the suffix *ti*, and the pron. *ma*.

61. *dhub*, sing. construct of the subst. *dhubu ;* Heb. טוב (see line 62).

    libbi, gen. sing. of *libbu* "heart ;" Heb לֵב.

62. *casad*, sing. masc. construct of *casadu* "a possession," from *casadu* "to conquer."

    irninte, gen. sing. of the collective *irnintu* (as above) ; "possession of the battle-cry" = "victory in battle."

    dhābis, adverb in -*is* from *dhabu* "good" (as in line 61). *Dhābu* is for *dhăvăbu*.

    lidhdharru, 3rd pl. masc. prec. Kal of *nadharu* "to guard ;" Heb. נטר.

64. *ikhabbu'u*, 3rd sing. masc. future Kal of *khabū* "to hide ;" Heb. הבא. (For the form see my *Assyrian Grammar*, pp. 52, 53, 69).

    isâpanu for *isappanu*, 3rd sing. masc. fut. Kal of *sapanu* "to sweep away," with *a* for *i* in the 3rd syllable ; Cp. Heb. ספה.

65. *me*, pl. masc. of *mu* "a drop of water." The reduplicated pl. *mami* also occurs ; Heb. מים.

    inâdu'u for *inaddu'u*, 3rd sing. masc. fut. Kal of *nadu'u* "to place ;" Cp. Ar. نَدَ.

66. *'isati*, pl. gen. fem. of *'isu* "fire" (Heb. אש).

    ikallu'u, 3rd sing. masc. fut. Kal of כלה "to burn" (as in Heb. and Ar.)

67. *epiri*, pl. of *ipru* or *epru* "dust ;" Heb. עפר.

    icâtumu for *icattumu*, 3rd sing. masc. fut. Kal of כתם, with *u* instead of *i* in the 3rd syllable.

    bil cummi (?). Conjectural transliteration. The first ideograph is "house" (*bitu*), the second "high" or "precious" (*ellu*), and the third "god" (*'ilu*). The second and third, however, must be taken together as a compound ideograph, and perhaps denote the Assyrian Plutus.

68. *lâ amari; lâ* "not" (Heb. לֹא), *amari,* the gen. masc. pl. after construct *asar* of the adjective *amaru* "seen;" therefore literally "things seen" (Cp. Heb. אוּר).

pisiris, adverb, in *-is* from *pisiru* "an interpretation" (Heb. and Aram. פשר).

inácimu for *inaccimu,* 3rd sing. masc. fut. Kal of נכם "to take."

69. *ipásidhu* for *ipassidhu,* 3rd sing. masc. fut. Kal of *pasadhu* "to strip" (Heb. פשט).

70. *isadharu* for *isadhdharu* (with *a* for *i*), 3rd sing. masc. fut. Kal of *sadharu* (as above).

milimma, acc. sing. of *milimma* or *milimmu,* from לוה "to cleave to." A variant reading gives *lumima* or *luviva,* apparently from the same root.

71. *limna,* acc. sing. masc. of the adj. *limnu* (for *limunu*), agreeing with *milimma;* perhaps akin to Heb. (and Ar.) לחם "to fight."

ikhasasa-va for *ikhassasa,* 3rd sing. masc. fut. Kal of *khasasu,* with final *u* changed to *-a* through the influence of the same vowel in both the following and the preceding syllables; Cp. Æth., *khasasa* "to investigate;" Ar. *khassa.*

72. *pān,* construct of *pānu* "face;" Heb. פנים.

73. *yusapracu,* 3rd sing. masc. fut. Shaphel of פרך "to break."

75. *'izzis,* adverb in *-is,* from *'izzu* "strong;" Heb. עז.

licálmu, 3rd pl. masc. prec. Pael of כלם "to injure" or "revile," contracted from *licallimu.*

76. *'arráti,* sing. fem. subst., from ארר "to curse" (see *liruru* below).

marusta for *marutsta,* fem. adj., agreeing with *'arrati,* from מרץ "to be violent" or "hard."

liruru, 3rd pl. masc. prec. Kal of ארר.

77. *sarrusu* for *sarrut-su; sarrut* fem. abstract sing. construct. Heb. שר "king."

liscibu, 3rd pl. masc. prec. Kal of *sacabu* "to pour out;" Ar. سكب

9*

78. *sul*, construct sing. of *sūlu* "ascent;" Shaphel pass. derivative of עלה "to ascend." The ideograph may also be read *isid* "foundation" (Heb. ויסד).

cussu, construct sing. of *cussu'u* "throne" (as in Heb.)

lisukhu for *lissukhu*, 3rd pl. masc. prec. Kal of כסה "to remove."

79. *tsabhi*, pl. construct of *tsabu* (Heb. צבא) "an army."

   luballu, 3rd pl. masc. prec. Pael of בלע "to devour."

80. *cacci*, pl. of *caccu* "a weapon;" perhaps for *carci* (Aram. כרך "armour ").

   lusabbiru, 3rd pl. masc. prec. Pael of שבר "to break."

81. *'abicti*, fem. abstract; Cp. Heb. הפך "to destroy."

   'ummani, gen. sing. fem. of *'ummanu* "army;" Cp. Heb. המון "multitude."

   liscunu, 3rd pers. masc. pl. prec. Kal of *sacanu* (as above).

82. *camis*, adverb in *-is*, from *camu*; Cp. Ar. كام.

83. *lusesibu*, 3rd pers. pl. masc. prec. Shaphel of *asibu* "to dwell;" Heb. ישב.

   simmi, gen. sing. masc. of *simmu* "a plague;" Cp. Heb. שמם.

84. *khulte*, adj. agreeing with *simmi*; Cp. Heb. חלה. The Semitic root seems to have been borrowed from Accadian.

   mat, construct sing. of *madu* or *mātu* "country," of Accadian origin (*ma-da*); Cp. Aram. מתא. (See line 86).

   libtsu, 3rd pl. masc. prec. Kal of בצע "to cut off."

85. *sunka*, acc. sing. of *sunku*; Cp. Talm. סנק "scantiness," "frugality."

   bubuta, acc. sing. of *bubutu* "crops;" perhaps Heb. ניב "fruit" may be compared. *Bubuta* is in opposition to *sunka*.

   khusakhkha, acc. sing. of *khusakhkhu* "need" (Aram. חשה).

86. *pagri*, acc. pl. masc. of *pagru* "a corpse" (Heb. פגר).

   matti for *madti* (or perhaps *māti*), gen. sing. of *mātu* (see line 84).

   liddi,' 3rd pers. sing. masc. prec. Kal of נדה (see above).

87. *malātisu* for *malātit-su*; *malātit*, construct of abstract in ית, from *malāti*, pl. fem., from מלא "to fill."

   likbi', 3rd sing. masc. prec. Kal of קבה (in Heb., "to curse").

88. *zir*, construct sing. of *zir'u* or *zer'u* "seed" (Heb. זרע).

   lukhallik, 3rd sing. masc. prec. Pael of חלק ("to divide," hence) "to scatter," "destroy."

THE LEGEND OF ISTAR.—OBVERSE.

The Cuneiform Characters to be supplied by the Student.

1. A-na mat NU-GA-A kak-ka-ri i-di-ya
To the land of Hades, regions of corruption,

2. D.P. Istaru banat D.P. Śini u-zu-un-sa [ci-nis]
Istar, daughter of the Moon-god, her attention [determinedly]

3. is - cun - va banat D.P. śini u - zu - un - [sa is - cun]
fixed, and the daughter of the Moon-god her attention fixed

4. a - na bit e - di - e su - bat 'il Ir - kal - la
(to go) to the house of corruption, the dwelling of the deity Irkalla;

5. a - na biti sa e - ri - bu - su la a - tsu - u
to the house whose entrance (is) without exit,

6. a - na khar - ra - ni sa a - lac - ta - su la ta - ai - rat (u)
to the road whose way (is) without return,

7. a - na biti sa e - ri - bu - su zu - um - mu - u mu - u - ra
to the house (at) whose entrance they bridle in the light;

8. a - sar epru mahdu bu - bu - uś - śu - nu a - cal - su - nu dhi - idh - dhu
a place (where) dust much (is) their food, their victuals (is) mud;

9. nu - u - ru ul im - ma - ru ina e - dhu - ti as - bā
(where) light not they see, in darkness they dwell; and

10. cal (?) - su - ma cima its - tsu - ri tsu - bat cap-pi
? like birds (is) the erecting of (their) wings;

11. eli dalti u sac - cul - sa mukh ep - ru
over the door and its wainscoting abundance of dust.

12. D.P. Istaru a - na bâbi D.P. NU-GA-A ina ca - sa - di - sa
Istar, to (at) the gate of Hades at her arrival

13. a - na ni - gab ba - a - bi a - ma - tuv iz - zac - car
to the porter of the gate (his) duty reminds;

14. a - na ni - gab me - c pi - ta ba - ab - ca
to the porter of the waters: Open thy gate!

15. pi - ta - a   ba - ab - ca - va   lu   ir - ru - ba   a - na - cu
    Open   *thy gate, and let   me enter in;*

16. sum - ma   la   ta - pat - ta - a   ba - a - bu   la   ir - ru - ba   a - na - cu
    if   not   thou openest   the gate (and) not   I enter in,

17. a - makh - kha - ats   dal - tuv   śic - cu - ru   a - sab - bir
    I force   the gate,   the bolt   I break,

18. a - makh - kha - ats   śi - ip - pu   va   u - sa - pal - cit   dalâti
    I force   the threshold, and I cross   the doors,

19. u - se - el - la   mi - tu - ti   acili   pal - dhu - ti
    I raise   the dead,   the devourers   of the living;

20. eli   pal - dhu - ti   i - ma - hi - du   mi - tu - ti
    above the   living   exceed   the dead.

ANALYSIS.

1. The Accadian MAD NU-GA-A is literally "land of the not returning,"
   ga'a being the participle of *gā* "to return" (see *Syllabary*). It is
   rendered in Ass. by *mat-la-naciri*. "The land from whence is no
   return" is a good name for Hades.
   kakkari, acc. pl. of *kakkaru*, Heb. כבּר (see my *Assyrian Grammar*, p. 29).
   êdi, written *êde* in line 4, gen. sing. of *êdu* "corruption," as Dr. Schrader has
   well explained it from עדה "to pass away."

2. *Istar*, the Hebrew Ashtoreth (Astarte), the Moon-goddess and Semitic
   Venus.
   bánat, construct sing. fem. of *banatu* (also *bintu*, i.e. *binitu*) "daughter"
   (Heb. בת). Sin, the Moon-god.
   'uzun, construct sing. of *'uzunu* or *'uznu* "ear" (Heb. אזן).
   cinis ?, supplied by Dr. Schrader, adverb in -*is* from adj. *cinu* (כון).

3. *iscun*, 3rd sing. masc. aor. of *sacanu*. It will be noticed that here as
   frequently elsewhere a feminine nominative is joined to a masc. verb.

4. *subat*, construct sing. fem. of *subǎtu* from ישב "to sit" or "dwell."

5. *eribu*, nom. sing. masc. infinitive (or verbal noun) from עָרַב "to enter" or "descend."

'atsu*, nom. sing. masc. verbal noun from יָצָא "to go out." The literal translation of the line is "of which its entering (there is) no outgoing."

6. *khar-ra-ni*, sing. oblique case of *kharranu*, a word originally borrowed from Accadian, which gave a name to the city of Kharran or Haran (Gen. xi. 31, &c.)

'alacta* or *halacta*, sing. fem. of *halactu* from הָלַךְ "to go."

tairat for *tairatu* (as often in the case of characters which denote syllables beginning and ending with a consonant), for *tayartu*, sing. fem. from תּוּר "to return."

7. *zummu*, 3rd pl. masc. (used impersonally) Permansive (or Perfect) Palel of זוּם. Cp. Targ. זְמַם "bridle." In Ass. *zumani* "impassable" is used of roads.

nura, acc. sing. of *nuru* "light" (so in Heb. [נֵר], Aram. and Ar.)

8. 'asar* "a place" (*see above*) often has the relative *sa* ("in which," "where") understood after it.

mahdu, nom. sing. masc. adj. agreeing with *epru*. Cp. Heb. מֵאד.

bubuśśunu for *bubut-sunu* (*see above*).

'acal*, construct sing. of the verbal noun *ácalu* "food," from אָכַל "to eat."

dhidhdhu, nom. sing. in opposition to *acal*. Heb. טִיט.

9. *immaru*, 3rd pers. pl. masc. present Kal of נָמַר, contracted from *inammaru*.

edhuti, gen. sing. of *edhutu* "darkness," from עָטָה, "to hide," as Dr. Schrader has pointed out.

'asbâ*, contracted from *asbū-a* for *asbū-va*, 3rd pl. masc. Permansive (or Perfect) Kal of 'asabu*, contracted from 'asibu* (also *yasibu*), with the enclitic conjunction.

10. The first word I cannot read.

'itstsuri*, pl. masc. of 'itstsuru* "a bird" (Ar. عصفور, Heb. צִפּוֹר).

tsubat, construct sing. fem. of *tsubătu* "a placing," from יָצַב. The reading and meaning of the word, however, are uncertain.

cappi, pl. masc. of *cappu*, contracted from *canapu* (Heb. כָּנָף), the double letter resulting from the assimilation of the nasal.

11. *dalti*, gen. sing. fem. of *daltu* (for *dalătu*) "door." (So in Heb.)

saccul, construct sing. of *sacculu*, which Dr. Schrader has well compared with Ar. شَكْل "likeness." A Syllabary makes *mescalŭ* a synonyme of *daltu*.

mukh, construct sing. of *mukhkhu*, from the adjective *makh*, which was borrowed from Accadian.

12. *bâbi*, gen. sing. of *bâbu* "gate" (as in Heb., &c.)

casidi, gen. sing. masc. of the verbal noun *casadu* "a reaching," from *casadu* "to take;" Cp. Ar. كَسَٰ.

13. *nigab*, construct sing. masc. Dr. Schrader derives it from a root נקף "to go round."

'amātuv, sing. fem. for *'amantuv* "fealty," "duty;" Heb. אמת "faithfulness."

izzaccar, for *iztaccar*, 3rd sing. masc. present Iphteal of זכר.

14. *mê* "waters" (as above).

pitā, for *piti-a* with the augment of motion, 2nd sing. masc. imperative Kal of *patû* "to open;" Heb. פתח. See also next line.

15. *irruba*, 1st pers. sing. masc. aor. Kal with augment of motion, from *eribu*. The *ayin* of the first syllable is replaced by a reduplication of the 2nd radical.

16. *summa*, adverb, perhaps from שום "to place."

tapattā, 2nd pers. sing. present Kal with augment of motion, from *patā*.

17. *amakhkhats*, 1st pers. sing. pres. Kal of מחץ.

siccuru, sing. noun (a pael derivative) ; Cp. Aram. סכרא "bolt."

asabbir, 1st pers. sing. pres. Kal of שבר.

18. *sippu*, sing. noun ; Heb. סף.

usapalcit, 1st pers. sing. aor. Shaphel of the quadriliteral *palcitu* ; Cp. Ar. قلب (?)

19. *usella*, 1st pers. sing. pres. Shaphel of עלה "to ascend," with *ll* on account of the *ayin*.

mitūti, pl. masc. part. pass. Kal of מות "to die."

'acili, pl. construct part. pres. Kal of *acalu*, "to eat."

paldhūti, pl. masc. part. Kal of *paladhu* or *baladhu*, "to live;" Cp. Heb. פלט.

20. *imahidu*, 3rd pers. pl. masc. pres. Kal of *mahadu* (whence *mahdu*, "much," line 7).

THE SACRIFICE OF CHILDREN (K 5139).

The transliteration to be supplied by the Student.

1. 𒀭 𒂊 𒐊 𒇉 𒂊 𒐊 𒂊
   ?   *may he remove, and*

2. 𒂊 𒐊 𒁹 𒐊 𒐊 𒐊 𒐊 𒂊 𒐊 𒅗 𒐊 𒐊 𒐊
   the   offspring   who   raises   the .head. among   men,

3. 𒂊 𒐊 𒐊 𒀭 𒀭 𒐊 𒐊 𒀭 𒐊 𒐊 𒐊 𒐊
   the   offspring   for   his   life   he   gave,

4. 𒐊 𒐊 𒂊 𒐊 𒐊 𒀭 𒐊 𒐊 𒐊 𒐊 𒐊 𒐊
   the head   of the offspring   for the head   of the man   he gave,

5. 𒐊 𒐊 𒂊 𒐊 𒐊 𒀭 𒐊 𒐊 𒐊 𒐊 𒐊
   the brow   of the offspring   for the brow   of the man   he gave,

6. 𒐊 𒐊 𒂊 𒐊 𒐊 𒀭 𒐊 𒐊 𒐊 𒐊 𒐊
   the breast   of the offspring   for the breast   of the man   he gave.

NOTES.

1. From נבט.

2. Cp. Ar. ورص "to bear eggs." Notice the correct use of the case-endings in this inscription.

   The Accadian SAK ILA (so *gadhu-la* is to be read), literally "head-raising," must be replaced by some corresponding Ass. adj. or part. of which -*u* is the phonetic complement. The Syllabaries render the words by *risa-nasû*.

   aveluti, abstract fem. sing.

5. *cisad* (see *casadi* above).

From the Hymn to Sin (K. 2861).

The English translation to be supplied by the Student.

1. bil - luv   e - bil - li   ili   sa   ina   same   u   irtsi - tiv

 e - dis - si - su   tsi - i - ru

2. a - bu   D.P. Na - an - nar   bel - luv   'ilu   dhabu   e - bil - li   ili

3. a - bu   D.P. Na - an - nar   bil - luv   i - lu   rab - u   e - bil - li   ili

4. a - bu   D.P. Na - an - nar   bil - luv   D.P. Sinu   e - bil - li   ili

5. a - bu   D.P. Na - an - nar   be - el   U - ri - e   e - bil - li   ili

6. a - bu   D.P. Na - an - nar   be - el   bit   samulli   e - bil - li   ili

7. a - bu   D.P.   Na - an - nar   be - el   a - gi - e   su - bu - u

 e - bil   li   ili

8. a - bu   D.P.   Na - an - nar   sa   sar - ru - tav   ra - bis   suc - lu - luv

 e - bil -   li   ili

9. a - bu   D.P.   Na - an - nar   sa   ina   ti - di - ic   ru - bu - tav

 i - nad - di - khu   e - bil -   li   ili

10.   bú - ru   ik - du   sa   kar - ni   gab - ba - ru   sa   mes - ri - ti

     suc - lu - luv   sic - ni   uc - ni - i   sac - nu

11.   cu - uz - bu - u   la - la - a   ma - lu - u

NOTES.

1. *ebilli*, 3rd pers. masc. aor. (with *i* termination) "he rules," from עָבַל another form of בְעַל.

   'edissi-su "he alone," anomalously formed from adverb *ĕdis*.

   tsīru, "supreme."

2. *Nannar*, "the luminary," a name of Sin, the Moon-god.

5. *Ure*, gen. of Ur, the city of Uru (now *Mugheir*).

6. *samulli* (in Accadian SIR-GAL) = "image." Heb. סֶמֶל.

7. *age* = "of crowns"; (the Semitic root was borrowed from Accadian).

   subū, Shaphel pass. part. of בוא "to come" (referring to the moon's motion).

8. *suclulu*, Shaphalel pass. part. of יכל "to be able," "to prevail."

9. *tidic*, construct sing. of a (Tiphel) noun with prefixed *t*, from *dācu* (= Heb. דכה).

   inaddikhu = "he will drive."

10. *bú'-ru*, or *buhru* = "brilliance" (as in Ar.)

   ikdu = "mighty" (of Accadian origin).

   mesriti = "the feet" or "limbs." Dr. Schrader compares the Heb. שִׁרְיָן "coat of mail," which in Aram. signifies "the artery" or "nerve."

   sicni = "habitations."

   ucnī = "marble" (probably of Accadian origin).

11. *cuzbū* = "beauty." Norris compares Heb. קֶצֶב.

   lalā = "fulness," from Accadian *lal*, "to fill" (see *Syllabary*).

HUNTING INSCRIPTIONS OF ASSUR-BANI-PAL (W.A.I. I, pl. 7).

The text to be transliterated by the Student.

1. 𒀭 . 𒀭 . ⟪ . I . ⟪ . 𒀭 . 𒅅 . 𒀭 .
   𒀭 . 𒀭 . 𒀭 .

2. 𒅅 . 𒅅 . V . 𒅅 .
   𒅅 . 𒅅 . V . 𒅅 . 𒅅 .

3. 𒅅 . I 𒅅 . 𒅅 . 𒅅 . 𒅅 . I .
   𒅅 . 𒅅 . 𒅅 . 𒅅 . 𒅅 . I 𒅅 .

NOTES.

1. 𒀭 "the good god," became the usual designation of Assur.

   𒀭 "the lady of the abyss," or "underworld," was a title of Beltis.

   'emuci, pl. of the substantive *'emucu*, "a deep intelligence," "a divinity" (Heb. עמק).

2. *yusatlimu's*, "they conferred on him," 3rd pl. masc. aor. Shaphel of *talamu*, with the possessive pronoun *s* contracted from *su*.

   𒅅 "great dog," was the Accadian name of "the lion" (Ass. *nesu*).

   adducu, Heb. דכה; notice the tense.

   𒅅 means "an altar," with the D.P. of *wood* and the phonetic complement *ānu*; but the reading of the ideograph is uncertain.

   izzitu, adj. ; Cp. Heb. עז.

   𒀭 "the goddess 15," symbol of Istar.

3. *azkup*, root זקף.

   mukhkhuru, "an offering," from מהר "to present."

   sun, contracted for *sunu*.

The text to be transliterated by the student.

1. 𒀭 𒁍 . (cuneiform text)

2. 𒌋 (cuneiform text)

3. 𒀸 (cuneiform text)

NOTES.

1. *multahti*, "renown," fem. abstract from the Iphteal part. of שאר "to make a noise," with *l* before *t* for *s*.

   issu, "fierce;" Cp. Heb. עסס (Aram. עסי) "to tread," "oppress."

2. *sa* = "of whom."

   tsir, "back" (Ar. ظهر).

   tuculti = "service."

   takhazi, weakened from *takhatsi*, for *takhkhatsi* (*tamkhatsi*) "battle," from מחץ.

3. D.P. *asmare*, "spears;" Cp. Heb. מסמר "a nail."

   aznik = "I pierced" (Cp. Heb. זק "a dart," זנק "to shoot forth"). The printed text gives *azkhul*, which must be wrong.

   zumur, "body;" ideograph of "body" or "skin," with phonetic complement *mur*. Delitzsch compares the Talmud צטורה "wind in the stomach."

The text to be transliterated by the Student.

1. 𒀯 𒀯 𒀯 . 𒀯 𒀯 𒀯 . 𒀯 . I . 𒀯 . 𒀯 𒀯 𒀯 .

2. 𒀯 𒀯 𒀯 𒀯 . 𒀯 𒀯 . 𒀯 . 𒀯 𒀯 . 𒀯 . 𒀯 . I . 𒀯 . 𒀯 𒀯 . 𒀯 𒀯 . 𒀯 .

3. 𒀯 . 𒀯 𒀯 . 𒀯 𒀯 𒀯 . 𒀯 𒀯 . 𒀯 𒀯 . 𒀯 𒀯 𒀯 . 𒀯 .

4. 𒀯 . 𒀯 𒀯 𒀯 𒀯 𒀯 . 𒀯 . 𒀯 . 𒀯 . 𒀯 𒀯 . 𒀯 . 𒀯 𒀯 𒀯 .

NOTES.

2. *melulti rubuti* "the action" or "right of sovereignty;" *melulti*, fem. abstract from עלל "to act" (especially "to act wonderfully").

3. *cibit* = "command" (with weakened guttural from קבה).

   𒀯 𒀯 𒀯 = Adar.

   𒀯 𒀯 = Nergal.

   ticli "ministers;" same root as *tucultu.*

4. D.P. *khutbale* = "ropes," Heb. חבל,

   mukhkha = "over" (of Accadian derivation).

   umatti', 1st pers. aor. Pael, "I stretched." Ar. خبل "to stretch a cord."

From the Black Obelisk of SHALMANESER (Layard's Insc. pl. 96 l. 159.)

The text to be transliterated by the Student.

159. 𒀭 ...

160. ...

161. ...

162. ...

163. ...

164. ...

165. ...

166. ...

167. ...

168. 𒀀𒀀𒀀 . 𒀀𒀀 . — . 𒀀𒀀𒀀 . 𒀀𒀀𒀀 . 𒀀𒀀𒀀 . 𒀀𒀀𒀀𒀀 .
𒀀𒀀𒀀 . 𒀀𒀀 . 𒀀𒀀 . 𒀀 . 𒀀𒀀𒀀𒀀 .
𒀀𒀀𒀀 .

169. 𒀀𒀀𒀀𒀀 . 𒀀𒀀𒀀𒀀𒀀 . 𒀀𒀀 . 𒀀𒀀 . 𒀀 . 𒀀𒀀 .
𒀀𒀀𒀀 . 𒀀 . 𒀀𒀀𒀀𒀀 . 𒀀 . 𒀀𒀀 .

NOTES.

159. "In my 30 campaigns" = "In my 30th campaign."

The city of Calkhi represents the Calah of Scripture.

ci utsbacuni "when I was stopping," 1st pers. sing. Permansive Kal of וצב with conditional suffix *ni*.

Dayan-Assur, "Assur is judge," was the name of the Tartan ("strong chief") or generalissimo.

160. 𒀀𒀀𒀀 ("host-many") = "armies."

panat, pl. fem. construct of *pānu*.

umāhir "I urged on" (Heb. מהר).

The Upper Zab is here referred to.

161. *'cbir* "I crossed."

lib = "middle" (the heart being the middle of a thing).

Read *'alāni* from *alu* (Heb. אהל "tent"); the phonetic complement *ni* shows how the plural sign is to be read.

icdarrib, Iphteal of *carabu* "to approach" (Heb. קרב), *t* being changed into *d* after *c*.

mādātu = "tribute," literally "gift;" for *mandattu* (*mandantu*), from *nadanu* (Heb. נתן).

162. *attakhar* "I received;" Iphteal of מחר.

163. *attusir* "I departed;" Ittaphal of וסר, another form of *vassaru* "to leave" (Cp. Heb. מסר).

165. These are the Minni of the Old Testament.
namurrat, fem. sing. construct from *namaru* "to see."

166. *ippar* "he fled;" Cp. Heb. עבר, *p* in Assyrian replacing *b*.
uvaśśir; see line 163.
suzub, Shaphel pass. verbal noun from עוב "to save."
napisti "life;" the plural sign is not to be read in Assyrian.
eli "he went up" from עלה,

167. *artedi*, Iphteal from רדה (Heb. ירד) "to descend."
sāsu "spoil" (Cp. Heb. שסה).
mani = "countable number." (Heb. מנה).

168. *abbal* "I strew down" (Heb. נפל),
āgur for *aggur* "I dug up" (Heb. נקר).
asrup "I burned" (Heb. שרף).

169. *limetu* from לוה "to cleave to."
acsud "I took," with phonetic complement *ud*.

www.ingramcontent.com/pod-product-compliance
Lightning Source LLC
Chambersburg PA
CBHW030604270326
41927CB00007B/1037